TALKS

BY 'ABDU'L-BAHÁ

TALKS

BY 'ABDU'L-BAHÁ

THE
EXISTENCE
OF GOD

Bahá'í
PUBLISHING
Wilmette, Illinois

Bahá'í Publishing
415 Linden Avenue, Wilmette, Illinois 60091-2844
Copyright © 2012 by the National Spiritual Assembly of
the Bahá'ís of the United States

15   14   13   12   4   3   2   1

Library of Congress Cataloging-in-Publication Data
'Abdu'l-Bah?, 1844–1921.
  [Speeches. English. Selections.]
  Talks by 'Abdu'l-Bah? : the existence of God / 'Abdu'l-Bah?.
      p. cm.
  Includes bibliographical references.
  ISBN 978-1-61851-001-3 (alk. paper)
  1. God. 2. Bahai Faith—Doctrines. I. Title. II. Title: Existence of God.
BP363.A3 2012
297.9'3824—dc23
                          2012000851

Cover design by Andrew Johnson
Book design by Patrick Falso

TALKS

BY 'ABDU'L-BAHÁ

Introduction

In 1912, a man known as 'Abdu'l-Bahá arrived on the shores of North America. He was sixty-seven years of age and had spent the majority of his life as a prisoner of the Ottoman Empire. At the time of his visit, he was the head of a little-known religion called the Bahá'í Faith. Few people in the Western world knew of the Faith he represented, and fewer still had ever heard his name. 'Abdu'l-Bahá's extraordinary visit to these shores had such a monumental impact on all those with whom he came in contact, however, that history continues to shed light on its significance.

The Bahá'í Faith, the newest of the independent world religions, was founded in 1844 in what is now Iran and owes its origin to the labors of two successive founding Prophets: the Báb and Bahá'u'lláh. As the Báb explained, His mission was to prepare the way for "Him Whom God shall make manifest," the Manifestation of God awaited by the followers of all faiths. During the course of successive waves of persecution that followed this announcement and that claimed the lives of the Báb and several thousands of

His followers, Bahá'u'lláh declared Himself to be the fulfillment of the divine promise.

'Abdu'l-Bahá (23 May 1844–28 November 1921) was the eldest surviving son and designated successor to Bahá'u'lláh, the Prophet-Founder of the Bahá'í Faith. Though he was known as "'Abbas Effendi" outside of the Bahá'í community, Bahá'ís often refer to him as "the Most Great Branch," "the Mystery of God," and "the Master"—titles bestowed on him by Bahá'u'lláh. After Bahá'u'lláh's passing in 1892, he chose to refer to himself as "'Abdu'l-Bahá," meaning "Servant of the Glory."

From the age of eight, 'Abdu'l-Bahá shared the exile and imprisonment of his father at the hands of the Ottoman Empire. Two years after finally being freed from prison at the age of sixty-seven, undeterred by poor health that was the result of a lifetime of hardship and suffering, he set out from Palestine (present-day Israel) on a momentous series of journeys throughout Europe and the United States. His purpose was to share the teachings and vision of Bahá'u'lláh with the people of the West. Over the course of his journeys, 'Abdu'l-Bahá gave a series of public addresses, which have been documented in a number of books. Speaking in Persian with the aid of a translator, he shared profound insights on a number of topics in a simple manner, accessible to anyone who listened with an open heart. 'Abdu'l-Bahá spoke on matters of spirituality as well as on the condition of the world. He shed light on complex matters of the soul and the spiritual nature of man, while addressing issues concerning society at large.

Collected in this third volume are talks that relate specifically to the proof of God's existence. During 'Abdu'l-Bahá's journey through the West, he spoke at many different and unique locations. One of the concepts he often proposed—particularly at universities and places of higher learning—was the undeniable proof of the existence of God, the Creator of our reality. Though God has been known by differing traditions and names throughout the ages, Bahá'ís believe that there is only one God and that He is the Creator of all things. Furthermore it is through the various Messengers of God, the Founders of the world's great religions, that we can come to know Him. In discussing our Creator, 'Abdu'l-Bahá also clarifies mankind's unique station in regard to the natural world. He introduces the concept of man having two natures: a lower nature, tied to the natural world, and a higher nature, granted to us by a knowing and loving God. It is through exercising this higher nature that man is enabled to draw closer to God by manifesting his innate nobility and reflecting the attributes of his Creator. It is hoped that readers enjoy these talks and are able to use them to help explain grand questions about existence and to understand fundamental realities of the world in which we reside.

2 May 1912

TALK AT
HOTEL PLAZA

Chicago, Illinois

Notes by Henrietta C. Wagner

When we carefully investigate the kingdoms of existence and observe the phenomena of the universe about us, we discover the absolute order and perfection of creation. The dull minerals in their affinities, plants and vegetables with power of growth, animals in their instinct, man with conscious intellect and the heavenly orbs moving obediently through limitless space are all found subject to universal law, most complete, most perfect. That is why a wise philosopher has said, "There is no greater or more perfect system of creation than that which already exists." The materialists and atheists declare that this order and symmetry is due to nature and its forces; that composition and decomposition which constitute life and existence are exigencies of nature; that man himself is an exigency of nature; that nature rules and governs creation; and that all existing things are captives of nature. Let us consider these statements. Inasmuch as we find all phenomena subject to an exact order and under control of universal law, the question is whether this is due to nature or to divine and omnipotent rule. The materialists believe that it is an exigency of nature for the rain to fall and that unless rain fell the earth would not become verdant. They reason that if clouds cause a downpour, if the sun sends forth heat and light and the earth is endowed with capacity, vegetation must inevitably follow; therefore, plant life is a property of these natural forces and is a sign of nature; just as combustion is the natural property of fire, therefore, fire burns, and we cannot conceive of fire without its burning.

In reply to these statements we say that from the premises advanced by materialists, the conclusions are drawn that nature is the ruler and governor of existence and that all virtues and perfections are natural exigencies and outcomes. Furthermore, it follows that man is but a part or member of that whereof nature is the whole.

Man possesses certain virtues of which nature is deprived. He exercises volition; nature is without will. For instance, an exigency of the sun is the giving of light. It is controlled—it cannot do otherwise than radiate light—but it is not volitional. An exigency of the phenomenon of electricity is that it is revealed in sparks and flashes under certain conditions, but it cannot voluntarily furnish illumination. An exigency or property of water is humidity; it cannot separate itself from this property by its own will. Likewise, all the properties of nature are inherent and obedient, not volitional; therefore, it is philosophically predicated that nature is without volition and innate perception. In this statement and principle we agree with the materialists. But the question which presents food for reflection is this: How is it that man, who is a part of the universal plan, is possessed of certain qualities whereof nature is devoid? Is it conceivable that a drop should be imbued with qualities of which the ocean is completely deprived? The drop is a part; the ocean is the whole. Could there be a phenomenon of combustion or illumination which the great luminary the sun itself did not manifest? Is it possible for a stone to possess inherent properties of which the aggregate mineral kingdom is lacking? For example, could the fingernail which is a part of human anatomy be endowed with cellular properties of which the brain is deprived?

Man is intelligent, instinctively and consciously intelligent; nature is not. Man is fortified with memory; nature does not possess it. Man is the discoverer of the mysteries of nature; nature is not conscious of those mysteries herself. It is evident, therefore, that man is dual in aspect: as an animal he is subject to nature, but in his spiritual or conscious being he transcends the world of material existence. His spiritual powers, being nobler and higher, possess virtues of which nature intrinsically has no evidence; therefore, they triumph over natural conditions. These ideal virtues or powers in man surpass or surround nature, comprehend natural laws and phenomena, penetrate the mysteries of the unknown and invisible and bring them forth into the realm of the known and visible. All the existing arts and sciences were once hidden secrets of nature. By his command and control of nature man took them out of the plane of the invisible and revealed them in the plane of visibility, whereas according to the exigencies of nature these secrets should have remained latent and concealed. According to the exigencies of nature electricity should be a hidden, mysterious power; but the penetrating intellect of man has discovered it, taken it out of the realm of mystery and made it an obedient human servant. In his physical body and its functions man is a captive of nature; for instance, he cannot continue his existence without sleep, an exigency of nature; he must partake of food and drink, which nature demands and requires. But in his spiritual being and intelligence man dominates and controls nature, the ruler of his physical being. Notwithstanding this, contrary opinions and materialistic views are set forth which would relegate man completely to physical subservience to nature's laws. This is equivalent to saying that the comparative degree exceeds the superlative, that the imperfect includes the perfect, that the pupil surpasses the teacher—all of which is illogical and impossible. When it is clearly manifest and evident that the intelligence of man, his constructive faculty, his power of penetration and discovery transcend nature, how can we say he is nature's thrall and captive? This would indicate that man is deprived of the bounties of God, that he is retrograding toward the station of the animal, that his keen superintelligence is without function and that he estimates himself as an animal, without distinction between his own and the animal's kingdom.

I was once conversing with a famous philosopher of the materialistic school in Alexandria. He was strongly opinionated upon the point that man and the other kingdoms of existence are under the control of nature and that, after all, man is only a social animal, often very much of an animal. When he was discomfited in argument, he said impetuously, "I see no difference between myself and the donkey, and I am not willing to admit distinctions which I cannot perceive." 'Abdu'l-Bahá replied, "No, I consider you quite different and distinct; I call you a man and the donkey but an animal. I perceive that you are highly intelligent, whereas the donkey is not. I know that you are well versed in philosophy, and I also know that the donkey is entirely deficient in it; therefore, I am not willing to accept your statement."

Consider the lady beside me who is writing in this little book. It seems a very trifling, ordinary matter; but upon intelligent reflection you will conclude that what has been written presupposses and proves the existence of a writer. These words have not written themselves, and these letters have not come together of their own volition. It is evident there must be a writer.

And now consider this infinite universe. Is it possible that it could have been created without a Creator? Or that the Creator and cause of this infinite congeries of worlds should be without intelligence? Is the idea tenable that the Creator has no comprehension of what is manifested in creation? Man, the creature, has volition and certain virtues. Is it possible that his Creator is deprived of these? A child could not accept this belief and statement. It is perfectly evident that man did not create himself and that he cannot do so. How could man of his own weakness create such a mighty being? Therefore, the Creator of man must be more perfect and powerful than man. If the creative cause of man be simply on the same level with man, then man himself should be able to create, whereas we know very well that we cannot create even our own likeness. Therefore, the Creator of man must be endowed with superlative intelligence and power in all points that creation involves and implies. We are weak; He is mighty, because, were He not mighty, He could not have created us. We are ignorant; He is wise. We are poor; He is rich. Otherwise, He would have been incapable of our creation.

Among the proofs of the existence of a divine power is this: that things are often known by their opposites. Were it not for darkness, light could not be sensed. Were it not for death, life could not be known. If ignorance did not exist, knowledge would not be a reality. It is necessary that each should exist in order that the other should have reality. Night and day must be in order that each may be distinguished. Night itself is an indication and evidence of day which follows, and day itself indicates the coming night. Unless night were a reality, there could not be day. Were it not for death, there could be no life. Things are known by their opposites.

Therefore, our weakness is an evidence that there is might; our ignorance proves the reality of knowledge; our need is an indication of supply and wealth. Were it not for wealth, this need would not exist; were it not for knowledge, ignorance would be unknown; were it not for power, there would be no impotence. In other words, demand and supply is the law, and undoubtedly all virtues have a center and source. That source is God, from Whom all these bounties emanate.

4 May 1912

TALK TO
THEOSOPHICAL
SOCIETY

NORTHWESTERN UNIVERSITY HALL
EVANSTON, ILLINOIS

Notes by Marzieh Moss

I am very happy in being present at this meeting. Praise be to God! I see before me the faces of those who are endowed with capacity to know and who desire to investigate truth. This is conducive to the greatest joy.

According to divine philosophy there are two important and universal conditions in the world of material phenomena: one which concerns life, the other concerning death; one relative to existence, the other nonexistence; one manifest in composition, the other in decomposition. Some define existence as the expression of reality or being and nonexistence as nonbeing, imagining that death is annihilation. This is a mistaken idea, for total annihilation is an impossibility. At most, composition is ever subject to decomposition or disintegration—that is to say, existence implies the grouping of material elements in a form or body, and nonexistence is simply the decomposing of these groupings. This is the law of creation in its endless forms and infinite variety of expression. Certain elements have formed the composite creature man. This composite association of the elements in the form of a human body is, therefore, subject to disintegration, which we call death, but after disintegration the elements themselves persist unchanged.

Therefore, total annihilation is an impossibility, and existence can never become nonexistence. This would be equivalent to saying that light can become darkness, which is manifestly untrue and impossible. As existence can never become nonexistence, there is no death for man; nay, rather, man is everlasting and ever-living. The rational proof of this is that the atoms of the material elements are transferable from one form of existence to another, from one degree and kingdom to another, lower or higher. For example, an atom of the soil or dust of earth may traverse the kingdoms from mineral to man by successive incorporations into the bodies of the organisms of those kingdoms. At one time it enters into the formation of the mineral or rock; it is then absorbed by the vegetable kingdom and becomes a constituent of the body and fibre of a tree; again it is appropriated by the animal, and at a still later period is found in the body of man. Throughout these degrees of its traversing the kingdoms from one form of phenomenal being to another, it retains its atomic existence and is never annihilated nor relegated to nonexistence.

Nonexistence, therefore, is an expression applied to change of form, but this transformation can never be rightly considered annihilation, for the elements of composition are ever present and existent as we have seen in the journey of the atom through successive kingdoms, unimpaired; hence, there is no death; life is everlasting. So to speak, when the atom entered into the composition of the tree, it died to the mineral kingdom, and when consumed by the animal, it died to the vegetable kingdom, and so on until its transference or transmutation into the kingdom of man; but throughout its traversing it was subject to transformation and not annihilation. Death, therefore, is applicable to a change or transference from one degree or condition to another. In the mineral realm there was a spirit of existence; in the world of plant life and organisms it reappeared as the vegetative spirit; thence it attained the animal spirit and finally aspired to the human spirit. These are degrees and changes but not obliteration, and this is a rational proof that man is everlasting, ever-living. Therefore, death is only a relative term implying change. For example, we will say that this light before me, having reappeared in another incandescent lamp, has died in the one and lives in the other. This is not death in reality. The perfections of the mineral are translated into the vegetable and from thence into the animal, the virtue always attaining a superlative degree in the upward change. In each kingdom we find the same virtues manifesting themselves more fully, proving that the reality has been transferred from a lower to a higher form and kingdom of being. Therefore, nonexistence is only relative and absolute nonexistence inconceivable. This rose in my hand will become disintegrated and its symmetry destroyed, but the elements of its composition remain changeless; nothing affects their elemental integrity. They cannot become nonexistent; they are simply transferred from one state to another.

Through his ignorance man fears death, but the death he shrinks from is imaginary and absolutely unreal; it is only human imagination.

The bestowal and grace of God have quickened the realm of existence with life and being. For existence there is neither change nor transformation; existence is ever existence; it can never be translated into nonexistence. It is gradation; a degree below a higher degree is considered as nonexistence. This dust beneath our feet, as compared with our being, is nonexistent. When the human body crumbles into dust, we can say it has become nonexistent; therefore, its dust in relation to living forms of human being is as nonexistent, but in its own sphere it is existent, it has its mineral being. Therefore, it is well proved that absolute nonexistence is impossible; it is only relative.

The purpose is this: that the everlasting bestowal of God vouchsafed to man is never subject to corruption. Inasmuch as He has endowed the phenomenal world with being, it is impossible for that world to become nonbeing, for it is the very genesis of God; it is in the realm of origination; it is a creational and not a subjective world, and the bounty descending upon it is continuous and permanent. Therefore, man, the highest creature of the phenomenal world, is endowed with that continuous bounty bestowed by divine generosity without cessation. For instance, the rays of the sun are continuous, the heat of the sun emanates from it without cessation; no discontinuance of it is conceivable. Even so, the bestowal of God is descending upon the world of humanity, never ceasing, continuous, forever. If we say that the bestowal of existence ceases or falters, it is equivalent to saying that the sun can exist with cessation of its effulgence. Is this possible? Therefore, the effulgences of existence are ever present and continuous.

The conception of annihilation is a factor in human degradation, a cause of human debasement and lowliness, a source of human fear and abjection. It has been conducive to the dispersion and weakening of human thought, whereas the realization of existence and continuity has upraised man to sublimity of ideals, established the foundations of human progress and stimulated the development of heavenly virtues; therefore, it behooves man to abandon thoughts of nonexistence and death, which are absolutely imaginary, and see himself ever-living, everlasting in the divine purpose of his creation. He must turn away from ideas which degrade the human soul so that day by day and hour by hour he may advance upward and higher to spiritual perception of the continuity of the human reality. If he dwells upon the thought of nonexistence, he will become utterly incompetent; with weakened willpower his ambition for progress will be lessened and the acquisition of human virtues will cease.

Therefore, you must thank God that He has bestowed upon you the blessing of life and existence in the human kingdom. Strive diligently to acquire virtues befitting your degree and station. Be as lights of the world which cannot be hid and which have no setting in horizons of darkness. Ascend to the zenith of an existence which is never beclouded by the fears and forebodings of nonexistence. When man is not endowed with inner perception, he is not informed of these important mysteries. The retina of outer vision, though sensitive and delicate, may, nevertheless, be a hindrance to the inner eye which alone can perceive. The bestowals of God which are manifest in all phenomenal life are sometimes hidden by intervening veils of mental and mortal vision which render man spiritually blind and incapable, but when those scales are removed and the veils rent asunder, then the great signs of God will become visible, and he will witness the eternal light filling the world. The bestowals of God are all and always manifest. The promises of heaven are ever present. The favors of God are all-surrounding, but should the conscious eye of the soul of man remain veiled and darkened, he will be led to deny these universal signs and remain deprived of these manifestations of divine bounty. Therefore, we must endeavor with heart and soul in order that the veil covering the eye of inner vision may be removed, that we may behold the manifestations of the signs of God, discern His mysterious graces and realize that material blessings as compared with spiritual bounties are as nothing. The spiritual blessings of God are greatest. When we were in the mineral kingdom, although we were endowed with certain gifts and powers, they were not to be compared with the blessings of the human kingdom. In the matrix of the mother we were the recipients of endowments and blessings of God, yet these were as nothing compared to the powers and graces bestowed upon us after birth into this human world. Likewise, if we are born from the matrix of this physical and phenomenal environment into the freedom and loftiness of the spiritual life and vision, we shall consider this mortal existence and its blessings as worthless by comparison.

In the spiritual world the divine bestowals are infinite, for in that realm there is neither separation nor disintegration, which characterize the world of material existence. Spiritual existence is absolute immortality, completeness and unchangeable being. Therefore, we must thank God that He has created for us both material blessings and spiritual bestowals. He has given us material gifts and spiritual graces, outer sight to view the lights of the sun and inner vision by which we may perceive the glory of God. He has designed the outer ear to enjoy the melodies of sound and the inner hearing wherewith we may hear the voice of our Creator. We must strive with energies of heart, soul and mind to develop and manifest the perfections and virtues latent within the realities of the phenomenal world, for the human reality may be compared to a seed. If we sow the seed, a mighty tree appears from it. The virtues of the seed are revealed in the tree; it puts forth branches, leaves, blossoms, and produces fruits. All these virtues were hidden and potential in the seed. Through the blessing and bounty of cultivation these virtues became apparent. Similarly, the merciful God, our Creator, has deposited within human realities certain latent and potential virtues. Through education and culture these virtues deposited by the loving God will become apparent in the human reality, even as the unfoldment of the tree from within the germinating seed. I will pray for you.

O Thou kind Lord! These are Thy servants who have gathered in this meeting, have turned unto Thy Kingdom and are in need of Thy bestowal and blessing. O thou God! Manifest and make evident the signs of Thy oneness which have been deposited in all the realities of life. Reveal and unfold the virtues which Thou hast made latent and concealed in these human realities.

O God! We are as plants, and Thy bounty is as the rain; refresh and cause these plants to grow through Thy bestowal. We are Thy servants; free us from the fetters of material existence. We are ignorant; make us wise. We are dead; make us alive. We are material; endow us with spirit. We are deprived; make us the intimates of Thy mysteries. We are needy; enrich and bless us from Thy boundless treasury. O God! Resuscitate us; give us sight; give us hearing; familiarize us with the mysteries of life, so that the secrets of Thy kingdom may become revealed to us in this world of existence and we may confess Thy oneness. Every bestowal emanates from Thee; every benediction is Thine.

Thou art mighty. Thou art powerful. Thou art the Giver, and Thou art the Ever-Bounteous.

31 October 1911

———————————

THE HOLY SPIRIT, THE INTERMEDIARY POWER BETWEEN GOD AND MAN

———————————

4 Avenue de Camoëns
Paris, France

The Divine Reality is Unthinkable, Limitless, Eternal, Immortal and Invisible.

The world of creation is bound by natural law, finite and mortal.

The Infinite Reality cannot be said to ascend or descend. It is beyond the understanding of man, and cannot be described in terms which apply to the phenomenal sphere of the created world.

Man, then, is in extreme need of the only Power by which he is able to receive help from the Divine Reality, that Power alone bringing him into contact with the Source of all life.

An intermediary is needed to bring two extremes into relation with each other. Riches and poverty, plenty and need: without an intermediary power there could be no relation between these pairs of opposites.

So we can say there must be a Mediator between God and Man, and this is none other than the Holy Spirit, which brings the created earth into relation with the "Unthinkable One," the Divine Reality.

The Divine Reality may be likened to the sun and the Holy Spirit to the rays of the sun. As the rays of the sun bring the light and warmth of the sun to the earth, giving life to all created beings, so do the

"Manifestations"* bring the power of the Holy Spirit from the Divine Sun of Reality to give light and life to the souls of men.

Behold, there is an intermediary necessary between the sun and the earth; the sun does not descend to the earth, neither does the earth ascend to the sun. This contact is made by the rays of the sun which bring light and warmth and heat.

The Holy Spirit is the Light from the Sun of Truth bringing, by its infinite power, life and illumination to all mankind, flooding all souls with Divine Radiance, conveying the blessings of God's Mercy to the whole world. The earth, without the medium of the warmth and light of the rays of the sun, could receive no benefits from the sun.

Likewise the Holy Spirit is the very cause of the life of man; without the Holy Spirit he would have no intellect, he would be unable to acquire his scientific knowledge by which his great influence over the rest of creation is gained. The illumination of the Holy Spirit gives to man the power of thought, and enables him to make discoveries by which he bends the laws of nature to his will.

The Holy Spirit it is which, through the mediation of the Prophets of God, teaches spiritual virtues to man and enables him to attain Eternal Life.

---

* The Manifestations of God, the Founders of the world's great religions.

All these blessings are brought to man by the Holy Spirit; therefore we can understand that the Holy Spirit is the Intermediary between the Creator and the created. The light and heat of the sun cause the earth to be fruitful, and create life in all things that grow; and the Holy Spirit quickens the souls of men.

The two great apostles, St Peter and St John the Evangelist, were once simple, humble workmen, toiling for their daily bread. By the Power of the Holy Spirit their souls were illumined, and they received the eternal blessings of the Lord Christ.

13 April 1912

TALK AT HOME OF MR. AND MRS. ALEXANDER MORTEN

---

141 East Twentyfirst Street

New York

Notes by Esther Foster

P raise be to God! This is a radiant gathering. The faces are brilliant with the light of God. The hearts are attracted to the Kingdom of Bahá.* I beg of God that day by day your faces may become brighter; day by day you may draw nearer to God; day by day you may take a greater portion from the outpourings of the Holy Spirit so that you may become encircled by the bounties of heaven.

The spiritual world is like unto the phenomenal world. They are the exact counterpart of each other. Whatever objects appear in this world of existence are the outer pictures of the world of heaven. When we look upon the phenomenal world, we perceive that it is divided into four seasons; one is the season of spring, another the season of summer, another autumn and then these three seasons are followed by winter. When the season of spring appears in the arena of existence, the whole world is rejuvenated and finds new life. The soul-refreshing breeze is wafted from every direction; the soul-quickening bounty is everywhere; the cloud of mercy showers down its rain, and the sun shines upon everything. Day by day

---

* *The kingdom of splendor*, the spiritual world in accordance with the teachings of Bahá'u'lláh.

we perceive that the signs of vegetation are all about us. Wonderful flowers, hyacinths and roses perfume the nostrils. The trees are full of leaves and blossoms, and the blossoms are followed by fruit. The spring and summer are followed by autumn and winter. The flowers wither and are no more; the leaves turn gray and life has gone. Then comes another springtime; the former springtime is renewed; again a new life stirs within everything.

The appearances of the Manifestations of God are the divine springtime. When Christ appeared in this world, it was like the vernal bounty; the outpouring descended; the effulgences of the Merciful encircled all things; the human world found new life. Even the physical world partook of it. The divine perfections were upraised; souls were trained in the school of heaven so that all grades of human existence received life and light. Then by degrees these fragrances of heaven were discontinued; the season of winter came upon the world; the beauties of spring vanished; the excellences and perfections passed away; the lights and quickening were no longer evident; the phenomenal world and its materialities conquered everything; the spiritualities of life were lost; the world of existence became like unto a lifeless body; there was no trace of the spring left.

Bahá'u'lláh has come into this world. He has renewed that springtime. The same fragrances are wafting; the same heat of the Sun is giving life; the same cloud is pouring its rain, and with our own eyes we see that the world of existence is advancing and progressing. The human world has found new life.

I hope that each and all of you may become like unto verdant and green trees so that through the breezes of the divine spring, the outpouring of heaven, the heat of the Sun of Truth, you may become eternally refreshed; that you may bear blossoms and become fruitful; that you may not be as fruitless trees. Fruitless trees do not bring forth fruits or flowers. I hope that all of you may become friends of the paradise of Abhá,* appearing with the utmost freshness and spiritual beauty. I pray in your behalf and beg of God confirmation and assistance.

---

* *The paradise of the most glorious,* the spiritual world beyond this world.

29 August 1912

———————————

TALK AT HOME OF MADAME MOREY

———————————

34 Hillside Avenue
Malden, Massachusetts

Notes by Edna McKinney

In the Books of the Prophets certain glad tidings are recorded which are absolutely true and free from doubt. The East has ever been the dawning point of the Sun of Reality. All the Prophets of God have appeared there. The religions of God have been promulgated, the teachings of God have been spread and the law of God founded in the East. The Orient has always been the center of lights. The West has acquired illumination from the East, but in some respects the reflection of the light has been greater in the Occident. This is especially true of Christianity. Christ appeared in Palestine, and His teachings were founded there. Although the doors of the Kingdom were opened in that country and the bestowals of Divinity were spread broadcast from its center, the people of the West have embraced and promulgated Christianity more fully than those in the East. The Sun of Reality shone forth from the horizon of the East, but its heat and ray are most resplendent in the West, where the radiant standard of Christ has been upraised. I have great hopes that the lights of Bahá'u'lláh's appearance may also find the fullest manifestation and reflection in these western regions, for the teachings of Bahá'u'lláh are especially applicable to the conditions of the people here. The western nations are endowed with the capability of understanding the rational and peerless words of Bahá'u'lláh and realizing that the essence of the teachings of all the former Prophets can be found in His utterance.

The teachings of Christ have been promulgated by Bahá'u'lláh, Who has also revealed new teachings applicable to present conditions in the world of humanity. He has trained the people of the East through the power and protection of the Holy Spirit, cemented the souls of humanity together and established the foundations of international unity.

Through the power of His words the hearts of the people of all religions have been attuned in harmony. For instance, among the Bahá'ís in Persia there are Christians, Muslims, Zoroastrians, Jews and many others of varying denominations and beliefs who have been brought together in unity and love in the Cause of Bahá'u'lláh. Although these people were formerly hostile and antagonistic, filled with hatred and bitterness toward each other, bloodthirsty and pillaging, considering that animosity and attack were the means of attaining the good pleasure of God, they have now become loving and filled with the radiant zeal of fellowship and brotherhood, the purpose of them all being service to the world of humanity, promotion of international peace, the unification of the divine religions and deeds of universal philanthropy. By their words and actions they are proving the verity of Bahá'u'lláh.

Consider the animosity and hatred existing today between the various nations of the world. What disagreements and hostilities arise, what warfare and contention, how much bloodshed, what injustice and tyranny! Just now there is war in eastern Turkey, also war between Turkey and Italy. Nations are devoted to conquest and bloodshed, filled with the animus of religious hatred, seeking the good pleasure of God by killing and destroying those whom in their blindness they consider enemies. How ignorant they are! That which is forbidden by God they consider acceptable to Him. God is love; God seeketh fellowship, purity, sanctity and long-suffering; these are the attributes of Divinity. Therefore, these warring, raging nations have arisen against Divinity, imagining they are serving God. What gross ignorance this is! What injustice, blindness and lack of realization! Briefly, we must strive with heart and soul in order that this darkness of the contingent world may be dispelled, that the lights of the Kingdom shall shine upon all the horizons, the world of humanity become illumined, the image of God become apparent in human mirrors, the law of God be well established and that all regions of the world shall enjoy peace, comfort and composure beneath the equitable protection of God. My admonition and exhortation to you is this: Be kind to all people, love humanity, consider all mankind as your relations and servants of the most high God. Strive day and night that animosity and contention may pass away from the hearts of men, that all religions shall become reconciled and the nations love each other so that no racial, religious or political prejudice may remain and the world of humanity behold God as the beginning and end of all existence. God has created all, and all return to God. Therefore, love humanity with all your heart and soul. If you meet a poor man, assist him; if you see the sick, heal him; reassure the affrighted one, render the cowardly noble and courageous, educate the ignorant, associate with the stranger. Emulate God. Consider how kindly, how lovingly He deals with all, and follow His example. You must treat people in accordance with the divine precepts—in other words, treat them as kindly as God treats them, for this is the greatest attainment possible for the world of humanity.

Furthermore, know ye that God has created in man the power of reason, whereby man is enabled to investigate reality. God has not intended man to imitate blindly his fathers and ancestors. He has endowed him with mind, or the faculty of reasoning, by the exercise of which he is to investigate and discover the truth, and that which he finds real and true he must accept. He must not be an imitator or blind follower of any soul. He must not rely implicitly upon the opinion of any man without investigation; nay, each soul must seek intelligently and independently, arriving at a real conclusion and bound only by that reality. The greatest cause of bereavement and disheartening in the world of humanity is ignorance based upon blind imitation. It is due to this that wars and battles prevail; from this cause hatred and animosity arise continually among mankind. Through failure to investigate reality the Jews rejected Jesus Christ. They were expecting His coming; by day and night they mourned and lamented, saying, "O God! Hasten Thou the day of the advent of Christ," expressing most intense longing for the Messiah; but when Christ appeared, they denied and rejected Him, treated Him with arrogant contempt, sentenced Him to death and finally crucified Him. Why did this happen? Because they were blindly following imitations, believing that which had descended to them as a heritage from their fathers and ancestors, tenaciously holding to it and refusing to investigate the reality of Christ. Therefore, they were deprived of the bounties of Christ, whereas if they had forsaken imitations and investigated the reality of the Messiah, they would have surely been guided to believing in Him. Instead of this they said, "We have heard from our fathers and have read in the Old Testament that Christ must come from an unknown place; now we find that this one has come from Nazareth." Steeped in the literal interpretation and imitating the beliefs of fathers and ancestors, they failed to understand the fact that although the body of Jesus came from Nazareth, the reality of the Christ came from the unknown place of the divine Kingdom. They also said that the scepter of Christ would be of iron—that is to say, He should wield a sword. When Christ appeared, He did possess a sword; but it was the sword of His tongue with which He separated the false from the true. But the Jews were blind to the spiritual significance and symbolism of the prophetic words. They also expected that the Messiah would sit upon the throne of David, whereas Christ had neither throne nor semblance of sovereignty; nay, rather, He was a poor man, apparently abject and vanquished; therefore, how could He be the veritable Christ? This was one of their most insistent objections based upon ancestral interpretation and teaching. In reality, Christ was glorified with an eternal sovereignty and everlasting dominion—spiritual and not temporal. His throne and Kingdom were established in human hearts, where He reigns with power and authority without end. Notwithstanding the fulfillment of all the prophetic signs in Christ, the Jews denied Him and entered the period of their deprivation because of their allegiance to imitations and ancestral forms.

Among other objections they said, "We are promised through the tongue of the prophets that Christ at the time of His coming would proclaim the law of the Torah, whereas now we see this person abrogating the commands of the Pentateuch, disturbing our blessed Sabbath and abolishing the law of divorce. He has left nothing of the ancient law of Moses; therefore, he is the enemy of Moses." In reality, Christ proclaimed and completed the law of Moses. He was the very helper and assister of Moses. He spread the Book of Moses throughout the world and established anew the fundamentals of the law revealed by Him. He abolished certain unimportant laws and forms which were no longer compatible with the exigencies of the time, such as divorce and plurality of wives. The Jews did not comprehend this, and the cause of their ignorance was blind and tenacious adherence to imitations of ancient forms and teachings; therefore, they finally sentenced Christ to death.

They, likewise, said, "Through the tongues of the prophets it was announced that during the time of Christ's appearance the justice of God would prevail throughout the world, tyranny and oppression would be unknown, justice would even extend to the animal kingdom, ferocious beasts would associate in gentleness and peace, the wolf and the lamb would drink from the same spring, the lion and the deer meet in the same meadow, the eagle and quail dwell together in the same nest; but instead of this, we see that during the time of this supposed Christ the Romans have conquered Palestine and are ruling it with extreme tyranny, justice is nowhere apparent, and signs of peace in the animal kingdom are conspicuously absent." These statements and attitudes of the Jews were inherited from their fathers—blind allegiance to literal expectations which did not come to pass during the time of Jesus Christ. The real purport of these prophetic statements was that various peoples, symbolized by the wolf and lamb, between whom love and fellowship were impossible would come together during the Messiah's reign, drink from the same fountain of life in His teachings and become His devoted followers. This was realized when peoples of all religions, nationalities and dispositions became united in their beliefs and followed Christ in humility, associating in love and brotherhood under the shadow of His divine protection. The Jews, being blind to this and holding to their bigoted imitations, were insolent and arrogant toward Christ and crucified Him. Had they investigated the reality of Christ, they would have beheld His beauty and truth.

God has given man the eye of investigation by which he may see and recognize truth. He has endowed man with ears that he may hear the message of reality and conferred upon him the gift of reason by which he may discover things for himself. This is his endowment and equipment for the investigation of reality. Man is not intended to see through the eyes of another, hear through another's ears nor comprehend with another's brain. Each human creature has individual endowment, power and responsibility in the creative plan of God. Therefore, depend upon your own reason and judgment and adhere to the outcome of your own investigation; otherwise, you will be utterly submerged in the sea of ignorance and deprived of all the bounties of God. Turn to God, supplicate humbly at His threshold, seeking assistance and confirmation, that God may rend asunder the veils that obscure your vision. Then will your eyes be filled with illumination, face to face you will behold the reality of God and your heart become completely purified from the dross of ignorance, reflecting the glories and bounties of the Kingdom.

Holy souls are like soil which has been plowed and tilled with much earnest labor, the thorns and thistles cast aside and all weeds uprooted. Such soil is most fruitful, and the harvest from it will prove full and plenteous. In this same way man must free himself from the weeds of ignorance, thorns of superstitions and thistles of imitations that he may discover reality in the harvests of true knowledge. Otherwise, the discovery of reality is impossible, contention and divergence of religious belief will always remain, and mankind, like ferocious wolves, will rage and attack each other in hatred and antagonism. We supplicate God that He may destroy the veils which limit our vision and that these becloudings, which darken the way of the manifestation of the shining lights, may be dispelled in order that the effulgent Sun of Reality may shine forth. We implore and invoke God, seeking His assistance and confirmation. Man is a child of God, most noble, lofty and beloved by God, his Creator. Therefore, he must ever strive that the divine bounties and virtues bestowed upon him may prevail and control him. Just now the soil of human hearts seems like black earth, but in the innermost substance of this dark soil there are thousands of fragrant flowers latent. We must endeavor to cultivate and awaken these potentialities, discover the secret treasure in this very mine and depository of God, bring forth these resplendent powers long hidden in human hearts. Then will the glories of both worlds be blended and increased and the quintessence of human existence be made manifest.

We must not be content with simply following a certain course because we find our fathers pursued that course. It is the duty of everyone to investigate reality, and investigation of reality by another will not do for us. If all in the world were rich and one man poor, of what use are these riches to that man? If all the world be virtuous and a man steeped in vice, what good results are forthcoming from him? If all the world be resplendent and a man blind, where are his benefits? If all the world be in plenty and a man hungry, what sustenance does he derive? Therefore, every man must be an investigator for himself. Ideas and beliefs left by his fathers and ancestors as a heritage will not suffice, for adherence to these are but imitations, and imitations have ever been a cause of disappointment and misguidance. Be investigators of reality that you may attain the verity of truth and life.

You have asked why it was necessary for the soul that was from God to make this journey back to God? Would you like to understand the reality of this question just as I teach it, or do you wish to hear it as the world teaches it? For if I should answer you according to the latter way, this would be but imitation and would not make the subject clear.

The reality underlying this question is that the evil spirit, Satan or whatever is interpreted as evil, refers to the lower nature in man. This baser nature is symbolized in various ways. In man there are two expressions: One is the expression of nature; the other, the expression of the spiritual realm. The world of nature is defective. Look at it clearly, casting aside all superstition and imagination. If you should leave a man uneducated and barbarous in the wilds of Africa, would there be any doubt about his remaining ignorant? God has never created an evil spirit; all such ideas and nomenclature are symbols expressing the mere human or earthly nature of man. It is an essential condition of the soil of earth that thorns, weeds and fruitless trees may grow from it. Relatively speaking, this is evil; it is simply the lower state and baser product of nature.

It is evident, therefore, that man is in need of divine education and inspiration, that the spirit and bounties of God are essential to his development. That is to say, the teachings of Christ and the Prophets are necessary for his education and guidance. Why? Because They are the divine Gardeners Who till the earth of human hearts and minds. They educate man, uproot the weeds, burn the thorns and remodel the waste places into gardens and orchards where fruitful trees grow. The wisdom and purpose of Their training is that man must pass from degree to degree of progressive unfoldment until perfection is attained. For instance, if a man should live his entire life in one city, he cannot gain a knowledge of the whole world. To become perfectly informed he must visit other cities, see the mountains and valleys, cross the rivers and traverse the plains. In other words, without progressive and universal education perfection will not be attained.

Man must walk in many paths and be subjected to various processes in his evolution upward. Physically he is not born in full stature but passes through consecutive stages of fetus, infant, childhood, youth, maturity and old age. Suppose he had the power to remain young throughout his life. He then would not understand the meaning of old age and could not believe it existed. If he could not realize the condition of old age, he would not know that he was young. He would not know the difference between young and old without experiencing the old. Unless you have passed through the state of infancy, how would you know this was an infant beside you? If there were no wrong, how would you recognize the right? If it were not for sin, how would you appreciate virtue? If evil deeds were unknown, how could you commend good actions? If sickness did not exist, how would you understand health? Evil is nonexistent; it is the absence of good. Sickness is the loss of health; poverty, the lack of riches. When wealth disappears, you are poor; you look within the treasure box but find nothing there. Without knowledge there is ignorance; therefore, ignorance is simply the lack of knowledge. Death is the absence of life. Therefore, on the one hand, we have existence; on the other, nonexistence, negation or absence of existence.

Briefly, the journey of the soul is necessary. The pathway of life is the road which leads to divine knowledge and attainment. Without training and guidance the soul could never progress beyond the conditions of its lower nature, which is ignorant and defective.

15 April 1912

———————

TALK AT
HOME OF
MOUNTFORT MILLS

———————

327 West End Avenue
New York

*Compiled from Stenographic Notes
by Howard MacNutt*

A few days ago I arrived in New York, coming direct from Alexandria. On a former trip I traveled to Europe, visiting Paris and London. Paris is most beautiful in outward appearance. The evidences of material civilization there are very great, but the spiritual civilization is far behind. I found the people of that city submerged and drowning in a sea of materialism. Their conversations and discussions were limited to natural and physical phenomena, without mention of God. I was greatly astonished. Most of the scholars, professors and learned men proved to be materialists. I said to them, "I am surprised and astonished that men of such perceptive caliber and evident knowledge should still be captives of nature, not recognizing the self-evident Reality."

The phenomenal world is entirely subject to the rule and control of natural law. These myriad suns, satellites and heavenly bodies throughout endless space are all captives of nature. They cannot transgress in a single point or particular the fixed laws which govern the physical universe. The sun in its immensity, the ocean in its vastness are incapable of violating these universal laws. All phenomenal beings—the plants in their kingdom, even the animals with their intelligence—are nature's subjects and captives. All live within the bounds of natural law, and nature is the ruler of all except man. Man is not the captive of nature, for although according to natural law he is a being of the earth, yet he guides ships over the ocean, flies through the air in airplanes, descends in submarines; therefore, he has overcome natural law and made it subservient to his wishes. For instance, he imprisons in an incandescent lamp the illimitable natural energy called electricity—a material force which can cleave mountains—and bids it give him light. He takes the human voice and confines it in the phonograph for his benefit and amusement. According to his natural power man should be able to communicate a limited distance, but by overcoming the restrictions of nature he can annihilate space and send telephone messages thousands of miles. All the sciences, arts and discoveries were mysteries of nature, and according to natural law these mysteries should remain latent, hidden; but man has proceeded to break this law, free himself from this rule and bring them forth into the realm of the visible. Therefore, he is the ruler and commander of nature. Man has intelligence; nature has not. Man has volition; nature has none. Man has memory; nature is without it. Man has the reasoning faculty; nature is deprived. Man has the perceptive faculty; nature cannot perceive. It is therefore proved and evident that man is nobler than nature.

If we accept the supposition that man is but a part of nature, we are confronted by an illogical statement, for this is equivalent to claiming that a part may be endowed with qualities which are absent in the whole.

For man who is a part of nature has perception, intelligence, memory, conscious reflection and susceptibility, while nature itself is quite bereft of them. How is it possible for the part to be possessed of qualities or faculties which are absent in the whole? The truth is that God has given to man certain powers which are supernatural. How then can man be considered a captive of nature? Is he not dominating and controlling nature to his own uses more and more? Is he not the very divinity of nature? Shall we say nature is blind, nature is not perceptive, nature is without volition and not alive, and then relegate man to nature and its limitations? How can we answer this question? How will the materialists and scholastic atheists prove and support such a supposition? As a matter of fact, they themselves make natural laws subservient to their own wish and purpose. The proof is complete that in man there is a power beyond the limitations of nature, and that power is the bestowal of God.

In New York I find the people more endowed with spiritual susceptibilities. They are not mere captives of nature's control; they are rising out of the bonds and burden of captivity. For this reason I am very happy and hopeful that, God willing, in this populous country, in this vast continent of the West, the virtues of the world of humanity shall become resplendent; that the oneness of human world-power, the love of God, may enkindle the hearts, and that international peace may hoist its standards, influencing all other regions and countries from here. This is my hope.

TALK AT
GREEN ACRE

Eliot, Maine

Notes by Edna McKinney

Are you all well and happy? This is a delightful spot; the scenery is beautiful, and an atmosphere of spirituality haloes everything. In the future, God willing, Green Acre shall become a great center, the cause of the unity of the world of humanity, the cause of uniting hearts and binding together the East and the West. This is my hope.

Tonight I wish to speak upon the oneness of the world of humanity. This is one of the important subjects of the present period. If the oneness of the human world were established, all the differences which separate mankind would be eradicated. Strife and warfare would cease, and the world of humanity would find repose. Universal peace would be promoted, and the East and West would be conjoined in a strong bond. All men would be sheltered beneath one tabernacle. Native lands would become one; races and religions would be unified. The people of the world would live together in harmony, and their well-being would be assured.

From the beginning of human history down to the present time the various religions of the world have anathematized and accused each other of falsity. Each religion has considered the others bereft of the face of God, deprived of His mercy and in the direct line of divine wrath. Therefore, they have shunned each other most rigidly, exercising mutual animosity and rancor. Consider the record of religious warfare, the battles between nations, the bloodshed and destruction in the name of religion. One of the greatest religious wars, the Crusades, extended over a period of two hundred years. In this succession of great campaigns the western crusaders were constantly invading the Orient, bent upon recovering the Holy City from the hands of the Islamic people. Army after army raised in Europe poured its fanatical legions into the East. The kings of European nations personally led these Crusades, killing and shedding the blood of the Orientals. During this period of two hundred years the East and West were in a state of violence and commotion. Sometimes the crusaders were successful, killing, pillaging and taking captive the Muslim people; sometimes the Muslims were victorious, inflicting bloodshed, death and ruin in turn upon the invaders. So they continued for two centuries, alternately fighting with fury and relaxing from weakness, until the European religionists withdrew from the East, leaving ashes of desolation behind them and finding their own nations in a condition of turbulence and upheaval. Hundreds of thousands of human beings were killed and untold wealth wasted in this fruitless religious warfare. How many fathers mourned the loss of their sons! How many mothers and wives lamented the absence of their dear ones! Yet this was only one of the "holy" wars. Consider and reflect.

Religious wars have been many. Nine hundred thousand martyrs to the Protestant cause was the record of conflict and difference between that sect of Christians and the Catholics. Consult history and confirm this. How many languished in prisons! How merciless the treatment of captives! All in the name of religion! Consider and estimate the outcome of other wars between the people and sects of religious belief.

From the beginning of human history down to this time the world of humanity has not enjoyed a day of absolute rest and relaxation from conflict and strife. Most of the wars have been caused by religious prejudice, fanaticism and sectarian hatred. Religionists have anathematized religionists, each considering the other as deprived of the mercy of God, abiding in gross darkness and the children of Satan. For example, the Christians and Muslims considered the Jews satanic and the enemies of God. Therefore, they cursed and persecuted them. Great numbers of Jews were killed, their houses burned and pillaged, their children carried into captivity. The Jews in turn regarded the Christians as infidels and the Muslims as enemies and destroyers of the law of Moses. Therefore, they call down vengeance upon them and curse them even to this day.

Consider what injuries, ordeals and calamities have been inflicted upon mankind since the beginning of history. Every city, country, nation and people has been subjected to the destruction and havoc of war. Each one of the divine religions considers itself as belonging to a goodly and blessed tree, the tree of the Merciful, and all other religious systems as belonging to a tree of evil, the tree of Satan. For this reason they heap execration and abuse upon each other. This is clearly apparent in books of historical record and prevailed until the time of the appearance of Bahá'u'lláh.

When the light of Bahá'u'lláh dawned from the East, He proclaimed the promise of the oneness of humanity. He addressed all mankind, saying, "Ye are all the fruits of one tree. There are not two trees: one a tree of divine mercy, the other the tree of Satan." Again He said, "Ye are all the fruits of one tree, the leaves of one branch." This was His announcement; this was His promise of the oneness of the world of humanity. Anathema and execration were utterly abrogated. He said, "It is not becoming in man to curse another; it is not befitting that man should attribute darkness to another; it is not meet that one human being should consider another human being as bad; nay, rather, all mankind are the servants of one God; God is the Father of all; there is not a single exception to that law. There are no people of Satan; all belong to the Merciful. There is no darkness; all is light. All are the servants of God, and man must love humanity from his heart. He must, verily, behold humanity as submerged in the divine mercy."

Bahá'u'lláh has made no exception to this rule. He said that among mankind there may be those who are ignorant; they must be trained. Some are sick; they must be treated. Some are immature; they must be helped to attain maturity. In other respects humanity is submerged in the ocean of divine mercy. God is the Father of all. He educates, provides for and loves all; for they are His servants and His creation. Surely the Creator loves His creatures. It would be impossible to find an artist who does not love his own production. Have you ever seen a man who did not love his own actions? Even though they be bad actions, he loves them. How ignorant, therefore, the thought that God, Who created man, educated and nurtured him, surrounded him with all blessings, made the sun and all phenomenal existence for his benefit, bestowed upon him tenderness and kindness and then did not love him. This is palpable ignorance, for no matter to what religion a man belongs, even though he be an atheist or materialist, nevertheless, God nurtures him, bestows His kindness and sheds upon him His light. How then can we believe God is wrathful and unloving? How can we even imagine this, when as a matter of fact we are witnesses of the tenderness and mercy of God upon every hand? All about us we behold manifestations of the love of God. If, therefore, God be loving, what should we do? We have nothing else to do but to emulate Him. Just as God loves all and is kind to all, so must we really love and be kind to everybody. We must consider none bad, none worthy of detestation, no one as an enemy. We must love all; nay, we must consider everyone as related to us, for all are the servants of one God. All are under the instructions of one Educator. We must strive day and night that love and amity may increase, that this bond of unity may be strengthened, that joy and happiness may more and more prevail, that in unity and solidarity all mankind may gather beneath the shadow of God, that people may turn to God for their sustenance, finding in Him the life that is everlasting. Thus may they be confirmed in the Kingdom of God and live forever through His grace and bounty.

Bahá'u'lláh has clearly said in His Tablets that if you have an enemy, consider him not as an enemy. Do not simply be long-suffering; nay, rather, love him. Your treatment of him should be that which is becoming to lovers. Do not even say that he is your enemy. Do not see any enemies. Though he be your murderer, see no enemy. Look upon him with the eye of friendship. Be mindful that you do not consider him as an enemy and simply tolerate him, for that is but stratagem and hypocrisy. To consider a man your enemy and love him is hypocrisy. This is not becoming of any soul. You must behold him as a friend. You must treat him well. This is right.

We return to the subject. When we observe the phenomena of the universe, we realize that the axis around which life revolves is love, while the axis around which death and destruction revolve is animosity and hatred. Let us view the mineral kingdom. Here we see that if attraction did not exist between the atoms, the composite substance of matter would not be possible. Every existent phenomenon is composed of elements and cellular particles. This is scientifically true and correct. If attraction did not exist between the elements and among the cellular particles, the composition of that phenomenon would never have been possible. For instance, the stone is an existent phenomenon, a composition of elements. A bond of attraction has brought them together, and through this cohesion of ingredients this petrous object has been formed. This stone is the lowest degree of phenomena, but nevertheless within it a power of attraction is manifest without which the stone could not exist. This power of attraction in the mineral world is love, the only expression of love the stone can manifest.

Look now upon the next highest stage of life, the vegetable kingdom. Here we see that the plant is the result of cohesion among various elements, just as the mineral is in its kingdom; but, furthermore, the plant has the power of absorption from the earth. This is a higher degree of attraction which differentiates the plant from the mineral. In the kingdom of the vegetable this is an expression of love, the highest capacity of expression the vegetable possesses. By this power of attraction, or augmentation, the plant grows day by day. Therefore, in this kingdom, also, love is the cause of life. If repulsion existed among the elements instead of attraction, the result would be disintegration, destruction and nonexistence. Because cohesion exists among the elements and cellular attraction is manifest, the plant appears. When this attraction is dispelled and the ingredients separate, the plant ceases to exist.

Then we come to the animal world, which is still higher in degree than the vegetable kingdom. In it the power of love makes itself still more manifest. The light of love is more resplendent in the animal kingdom because the power of attraction whereby elements cohere and cellular atoms commingle now reveals itself in certain emotions and sensibilities which produce instinctive fellowship and association. The animals are imbued with kindness and affinity which manifests itself among those of the same species.

Finally, we reach the kingdom of man. Here we find that all the degrees of the mineral, vegetable and animal expressions of love are present plus unmistakable attractions of consciousness. That is to say, man is the possessor of a degree of attraction which is conscious and spiritual. Here is an immeasurable advance. In the human kingdom spiritual susceptibilities come into view, love exercises its superlative degree, and this is the cause of human life.

The proof is clear that in all degrees and kingdoms unity and agreement, love and fellowship are the cause of life, whereas dissension, animosity and separation are ever conducive to death. Therefore, we must strive with life and soul in order that day by day unity and agreement may be increased among mankind and that love and affinity may become more resplendently glorious and manifest. In the animal kingdom you will observe that domestic species live together in the utmost fellowship. See how sociable and friendly sheep gather together in a flock. Look at the doves and other domestic birds. There is no partisanship among them, no separation due to notions of patriotism. They live together in the utmost love and unity, flying, feeding, associating. Ferocious animals—beasts of prey such as the wolf, bear, tiger and hyena—are never amicable and do not associate together. They attack one another. Whenever they meet, they fight. Three wolves are never seen associating happily. If you see them together, it is with some ferocious intent. They are like selfish, brutal men who are inimical, cursing and killing each other. Better that man should resemble the domestic animals than the ferocious beasts of prey, for in the estimation of God love is acceptable, whereas hatred and animosity are rejected. Why should we act contrary to the good pleasure of God? Why should we be as ferocious animals, constantly shedding blood, pillaging and destroying? Because we belong to one race or family of humankind, why should we consider all others bad and inferior, deserving of death, pillage and invasion—people of darkness, worthy of hatred and detestation by God? Why does man show forth such attitude and actions toward his fellowman? We see that God is kind to all. Just as He loves us, He loves all others; just as He provides for us, He provides for the rest. He nurtures and trains all with equal solicitude.

God is great! God is kind! He does not behold human shortcomings; He does not regard human weaknesses. Man is a creature of His mercy, and to His mercy He summons all. Why then should we despise or detest His creatures because this one is a Jew, another a Buddhist or Zoroastrian and so on? This is ignorance, for the oneness of humanity as servants of God is an assured and certain fact.

Bahá'u'lláh has proclaimed the promise of the oneness of humanity. Therefore, we must exercise the utmost love toward each other. We must be loving to all the people of the world. We must not consider any people the people of Satan, but know and recognize all as the servants of the one God. At most it is this: Some do not know; they must be guided and trained. They must be taught to love their fellow creatures and be encouraged in the acquisition of virtues. Some are ignorant; they must be informed. Some are as children, undeveloped; they must be helped to reach maturity. Some are ailing, their moral condition is unhealthy; they must be treated until their morals are purified. But the sick man is not to be hated because he is sick, the child must not be shunned because he is a child, the ignorant one is not to be despised because he lacks knowledge. They must all be treated, educated, trained and assisted in love. Everything must be done in order that humanity may live under the shadow of God in the utmost security, enjoying happiness in its highest degree.

———————

TALK AT FOURTH ANNUAL CONFERENCE OF THE NATIONAL ASSOCIATION FOR THE ADVANCEMENT OF COLORED PEOPLE

———————

HANDEL HALL
CHICAGO, ILLINOIS

Notes by Joseph H. Hannen

According to the words of the Old Testament God has said, "Let us make man in our image, after our likeness." This indicates that man is of the image and likeness of God—that is to say, the perfections of God, the divine virtues, are reflected or revealed in the human reality. Just as the light and effulgence of the sun when cast upon a polished mirror are reflected fully, gloriously, so, likewise, the qualities and attributes of Divinity are radiated from the depths of a pure human heart. This is an evidence that man is the most noble of God's creatures.

Each kingdom of creation is endowed with its necessary complement of attributes and powers. The mineral possesses inherent virtues of its own kingdom in the scale of existence. The vegetable possesses the qualities of the mineral plus an augmentative virtue, or power of growth. The animal is endowed with the virtues of both the mineral and vegetable plane plus the power of intellect. The human kingdom is replete with the perfections of all the kingdoms below it with the addition of powers peculiar to man alone. Man is, therefore, superior to all the creatures below him, the loftiest and most glorious being of creation. Man is the microcosm; and the infinite universe, the macrocosm. The mysteries of the greater world, or macrocosm, are expressed or revealed in the lesser world, the microcosm. The tree, so to speak, is the greater world, and the seed in its relation to the tree is the lesser world. But the whole of the great tree is potentially latent and hidden in the little seed. When this seed is planted and cultivated, the tree is revealed. Likewise, the greater world, the macrocosm, is latent and miniatured in the lesser world, or microcosm, of man. This constitutes the universality or perfection of virtues potential in mankind. Therefore, it is said that man has been created in the image and likeness of God.

Let us now discover more specifically how he is the image and likeness of God and what is the standard or criterion by which he can be measured and estimated. This standard can be no other than the divine virtues which are revealed in him. Therefore, every man imbued with divine qualities, who reflects heavenly moralities and perfections, who is the expression of ideal and praiseworthy attributes, is, verily, in the image and likeness of God. If a man possesses wealth, can we call him an image and likeness of God? Or is human honor and notoriety the criterion of divine nearness? Can we apply the test of racial color and say that man of a certain hue—white, black, brown, yellow, red—is the true image of his Creator? We must conclude that color is not the standard and estimate of judgment and that it is of no importance, for color is accidental in nature. The spirit and intelligence of man is essential, and that is the manifestation of divine virtues, the merciful bestowals of God, the eternal life and baptism through the Holy Spirit. Therefore, be it known that color or race is of no importance. He who is the image and likeness of God, who is the manifestation of the bestowals of God, is acceptable at the threshold of God—whether his color be white, black or brown; it matters not. Man is not man simply because of bodily attributes. The standard of divine measure and judgment is his intelligence and spirit.

Therefore, let this be the only criterion and estimate, for this is the image and likeness of God. A man's heart may be pure and white though his outer skin be black; or his heart be dark and sinful though his racial color is white. The character and purity of the heart is of all importance. The heart illumined by the light of God is nearest and dearest to God, and inasmuch as God has endowed man with such favor that he is called the image of God, this is truly a supreme perfection of attainment, a divine station which is not to be sacrificed by the mere accident of color.

25 April 1912

TALK TO
THEOSOPHICAL
SOCIETY

Home of
Mr. and Mrs. Arthur J. Parsons
1700 Eighteenth Street
NW, Washington, D.C.

Notes by Joseph H. Hannen

The greatest power in the realm and range of human existence is spirit—the divine breath which animates and pervades all things. It is manifested throughout creation in different degrees or kingdoms. In the vegetable kingdom it is the augmentative spirit or power of growth, the animus of life and development in plants, trees and organisms of the floral world. In this degree of its manifestation spirit is unconscious of the powers which qualify the kingdom of the animal. The distinctive virtue or plus of the animal is sense perception; it sees, hears, smells, tastes and feels but is incapable, in turn, of conscious ideation or reflection which characterizes and differentiates the human kingdom. The animal neither exercises nor apprehends this distinctive human power and gift. From the visible it cannot draw conclusions regarding the invisible, whereas the human mind from visible and known premises attains knowledge of the unknown and invisible. For instance, Christopher Columbus from information based upon known and provable facts drew conclusions which led him unerringly across the vast ocean to the unknown continent of America. Such power of accomplishment is beyond the range of animal intelligence. Therefore, this power is a distinctive attribute of the human spirit and kingdom. The animal spirit cannot penetrate and discover the mysteries of things. It is a captive of the senses. No amount of teaching, for instance, would enable it to grasp the fact that the sun is stationary, and the earth moves around it. Likewise, the human spirit has its limitations. It cannot comprehend the phenomena of the Kingdom transcending the human station, for it is a captive of powers and life forces which have their operation upon its own plane of existence, and it cannot go beyond that boundary.

There is, however, another Spirit, which may be termed the Divine, to which Jesus Christ refers when He declares that man must be born of its quickening and baptized with its living fire. Souls deprived of that Spirit are accounted as dead, though they are possessed of the human spirit. Jesus Christ has pronounced them dead inasmuch as they have no portion of the Divine Spirit. He says, "Let the dead bury their dead." In another instance He declares, "That which is born of the flesh is flesh; and that which is born of the Spirit is spirit." By this He means that souls, though alive in the human kingdom, are nevertheless dead if devoid of this particular spirit of divine quickening. They have not partaken of the divine life of the higher Kingdom, for the soul which partakes of the power of the Divine Spirit is, verily, living.

This quickening spirit emanates spontaneously from the Sun of Truth, from the reality of Divinity, and is not a revelation or a manifestation. It is like the rays of the sun. The rays are emanations from the sun. This does not mean that the sun has become divisible, that a part of the sun has come out into space. This plant beside me has risen from the seed; therefore, it is a manifestation and unfoldment of the seed. The seed, as you can see, has unfolded in manifestation, and the result is this plant. Every leaf of the plant is a part of the seed. But the reality of Divinity is indivisible, and each individual of humankind cannot be a part of it as is often claimed. Nay, rather, the individual realities of mankind, when spiritually born, are emanations from the reality of Divinity, just as the flame, heat and light of the sun are the effulgence of the sun and not a part of the sun itself. Therefore, a spirit has emanated from the reality of Divinity, and its effulgences have become visible in human entities or realities. This ray and this heat are permanent. There is no cessation in the effulgence. As long as the sun exists, the heat and light will exist, and inasmuch as eternity is a property of Divinity, this emanation is everlasting. There is no cessation in its outpouring. The more the world of humanity develops, the more the effulgences or emanations of Divinity will become revealed, just as the stone, when it becomes polished and pure as a mirror, will reflect in fuller degree the glory and splendor of the sun.

The mission of the Prophets, the revelation of the Holy Books, the manifestation of the heavenly Teachers and the purpose of divine philosophy all center in the training of the human realities so that they may become clear and pure as mirrors and reflect the light and love of the Sun of Reality. Therefore, I hope that—whether you be in the East or the West—you will strive with heart and soul in order that day by day the world of humanity may become glorified, more spiritual, more sanctified; and that the splendor of the Sun of Reality may be revealed fully in human hearts as in a mirror. This is worthy of the world of mankind. This is the true evolution and progress of humanity. This is the supreme bestowal. Otherwise, by simple development along material lines man is not perfected. At most, the physical aspect of man, his natural or material conditions, may become stabilized and improved, but he will remain deprived of the spiritual or divine bestowal. He is then like a body without a spirit, a lamp without the light, an eye without the power of vision, an ear that hears no sound, a mind incapable of perceiving, an intellect minus the power of reason.

Man has two powers; and his development, two aspects. One power is connected with the material world, and by it he is capable of material advancement. The other power is spiritual, and through its development his inner, potential nature is awakened. These powers are like two wings. Both must be developed, for flight is impossible with one wing. Praise be to God! Material advancement has been evident in the world, but there is need of spiritual advancement in like proportion. We must strive unceasingly and without rest to accomplish the development of the spiritual nature in man, and endeavor with tireless energy to advance humanity toward the nobility of its true and intended station. For the body of man is accidental; it is of no importance. The time of its disintegration will inevitably come. But the spirit of man is essential and, therefore, eternal. It is a divine bounty. It is the effulgence of the Sun of Reality and, therefore, of greater importance than the physical body.

I pray for you. You have come to visit me, and I am most grateful. I shall ask confirmation and assistance for you from God, the Generous, the Bestower, that you may be aided in serving the world of humanity.

23 April 1912

_____

TALK AT
HOME OF
MR. AND MRS.
ARTHUR J. PARSONS

_____

1700 Eighteenth Street, NW
Washington, D.C.

Notes by Joseph H. Hannen

Today I have been speaking from dawn until now, yet because of love, fellowship and desire to be with you, I have come here to speak again briefly. Within the last few days a terrible event has happened in the world, an event saddening to every heart and grieving every spirit. I refer to the Titanic disaster, in which many of our fellow human beings were drowned, a number of beautiful souls passed beyond this earthly life. Although such an event is indeed regrettable, we must realize that everything which happens is due to some wisdom and that nothing happens without a reason. Therein is a mystery; but whatever the reason and mystery, it was a very sad occurrence, one which brought tears to many eyes and distress to many souls. I was greatly affected by this disaster. Some of those who were lost voyaged on the Cedric with us as far as Naples and afterward sailed upon the other ship. When I think of them, I am very sad indeed. But when I consider this calamity in another aspect, I am consoled by the realization that the worlds of God are infinite; that though they were deprived of this existence, they have other opportunities in the life beyond, even as Christ has said, "In my Father's house are many mansions." They

were called away from the temporary and transferred
to the eternal; they abandoned this material existence
and entered the portals of the spiritual world. Fore-
going the pleasures and comforts of the earthly, they
now partake of a joy and happiness far more abiding
and real, for they have hastened to the Kingdom of
God. The mercy of God is infinite, and it is our duty
to remember these departed souls in our prayers and
supplications that they may draw nearer and nearer to
the Source itself.

These human conditions may be likened to the
matrix of the mother from which a child is to be born
into the spacious outer world. At first the infant finds
it very difficult to reconcile itself to its new existence.
It cries as if not wishing to be separated from its narrow abode and imagining that life is restricted to that
limited space. It is reluctant to leave its home, but
nature forces it into this world. Having come into
its new conditions, it finds that it has passed from
darkness into a sphere of radiance; from gloomy and
restricted surroundings it has been transferred to a
spacious and delightful environment. Its nourishment
was the blood of the mother; now it finds delicious
food to enjoy. Its new life is filled with brightness and
beauty; it looks with wonder and delight upon the
mountains, meadows and fields of green, the rivers
and fountains, the wonderful stars; it breathes the
life-quickening atmosphere; and then it praises God
for its release from the confinement of its former con-

dition and attainment to the freedom of a new realm. This analogy expresses the relation of the temporal world to the life hereafter—the transition of the soul of man from darkness and uncertainty to the light and reality of the eternal Kingdom. At first it is very difficult to welcome death, but after attaining its new condition the soul is grateful, for it has been released from the bondage of the limited to enjoy the liberties of the unlimited. It has been freed from a world of sorrow, grief and trials to live in a world of unending bliss and joy. The phenomenal and physical have been abandoned in order that it may attain the opportunities of the ideal and spiritual. Therefore, the souls of those who have passed away from earth and completed their span of mortal pilgrimage in the Titanic disaster have hastened to a world superior to this. They have soared away from these conditions of darkness and dim vision into the realm of light. These are the only considerations which can comfort and console those whom they have left behind.

Furthermore, these events have deeper reasons. Their object and purpose is to teach man certain lessons. We are living in a day of reliance upon material conditions. Men imagine that the great size and strength of a ship, the perfection of machinery or the skill of a navigator will ensure safety, but these disasters sometimes take place that men may know that God is the real Protector. If it be the will of God to protect man, a little ship may escape destruction, whereas the greatest and most perfectly constructed vessel with the best and most skillful navigator may not survive a danger such as was present on the ocean. The purpose is that the people of the world may turn to God, the One Protector; that human souls may rely upon His preservation and know that He is the real safety. These events happen in order that man's faith may be increased and strengthened. Therefore, although we feel sad and disheartened, we must supplicate God to turn our hearts to the Kingdom and pray for these departed souls with faith in His infinite mercy so that, although they have been deprived of this earthly life, they may enjoy a new existence in the supreme mansions of the Heavenly Father.

Let no one imagine that these words imply that man should not be thorough and careful in his undertakings. God has endowed man with intelligence so that he may safeguard and protect himself. Therefore, he must provide and surround himself with all that scientific skill can produce. He must be deliberate, thoughtful and thorough in his purposes, build the best ship and provide the most experienced captain; yet, withal, let him rely upon God and consider God as the one Keeper. If God protects, nothing can imperil man's safety; and if it be not His will to safeguard, no amount of preparation and precaution will avail.

12 May 1912

_____

T A L K   A T
U N I T Y   C H U R C H

_____

Montclair, New Jersey

Notes by Esther Foster

I wish to speak upon the subject of divine unity, the oneness of God, before this revered assemblage.

It is a self-evident fact that phenomenal existence can never grasp nor comprehend the ancient and essential Reality. Utter weakness cannot understand absolute strength. When we view the world of creation, we discover differences in degree which make it impossible for the lower to comprehend the higher. For example, the mineral kingdom, no matter how much it may advance, can never comprehend the phenomena of the vegetable kingdom. Whatever development the vegetable may attain, it can have no message from nor come in touch with the kingdom of the animal. However perfect may be the growth of a tree, it cannot realize the sensation of sight, hearing, smell, taste and touch; these are beyond its limitation. Although it is the possessor of existence in the world of creation, a tree, nevertheless, has no knowledge of the superior degree of the animal kingdom. Likewise, no matter how great the advancement of the animal, it can have no idea of the human plane, no knowledge of intellect and spirit. Difference in degree is an obstacle to this comprehension. A lower degree cannot comprehend a higher although all are in the same world of creation—whether mineral, vegetable or animal. Degree is the barrier and limitation. In the human plane of existence we can say we have knowledge of a vegetable, its qualities and product; but the vegetable has no knowledge or comprehension whatever of us. No matter how near perfection this rose may advance in its own sphere, it can never possess hearing and sight. Inasmuch as in the creational world, which is phenomenal, difference of degree is an obstacle or hindrance to comprehension, how can the human being, which is a created exigency, comprehend the ancient divine Reality, which is essential? This is impossible because the reality of Divinity is sanctified beyond the comprehension of the created being, man.

Furthermore, that which man can grasp is finite to man, and man to it is as infinite. Is it possible then for the reality of Divinity to be finite and the human creature infinite? On the contrary, the reverse is true; the human is finite while the essence of Divinity is infinite. Whatever comes within the sphere of human comprehension must be limited and finite. As the essence of Divinity transcends the comprehension of man, therefore God brings forth certain Manifestations of the divine Reality upon Whom He bestows heavenly effulgences in order that They may be intermediaries between humanity and Himself. These holy Manifestations or Prophets of God are as mirrors which have acquired illumination from the Sun of Truth, but the Sun does not descend from its high zenith and does not effect entrance within the mirror. In truth, this mirror has attained complete polish and purity until the utmost capacity of reflection has been developed in it; therefore, the Sun of Reality with its fullest effulgence and splendor is revealed therein. These mirrors are earthly, whereas the reality of Divinity is in its highest apogee. Although its lights are shining and its heat is manifest in them, although these mirrors are telling their story of its effulgence, the Sun, nevertheless, remains in its own lofty station; it does not descend; it does not effect entrance, because it is holy and sanctified.

The Sun of Divinity and of Reality has revealed itself in various mirrors. Though these mirrors are many, yet the Sun is one. The bestowals of God are one; the reality of the divine religion is one. Consider how one and the same light has reflected itself in the different mirrors or manifestations of it. There are certain souls who are lovers of the Sun; they perceive the effulgence of the Sun from every mirror. They are not fettered or attached to the mirrors; they are attached to the Sun itself and adore it, no matter from what point it may shine. But those who adore the mirror and are attached to it become deprived of witnessing the light of the Sun when it shines forth from another mirror. For instance, the Sun of Reality revealed itself from the Mosaic mirror. The people who were sincere accepted and believed in it. When the same Sun shone from the Messianic mirror, the Jews who were not lovers of the Sun and who were fettered by their adoration of the mirror of Moses did not perceive the lights and effulgences of the Sun of Reality resplendent in Jesus; therefore, they were deprived of its bestowals. Yet the Sun of Reality, the Word of God, shone from the Messianic mirror through the wonderful channel of Jesus Christ more fully and more wonderfully. Its effulgences were manifestly radiant, but even to this day the Jews are holding to the Mosaic mirror. Therefore, they are bereft of witnessing the lights of eternity in Jesus.

In brief, the sun is one sun, the light is one light which shines upon all phenomenal beings. Every creature has a portion thereof, but the pure mirror can reveal the story of its bounty more fully and completely. Therefore, we must adore the light of the Sun, no matter through what mirror it may be revealed. We must not entertain prejudice, for prejudice is an obstacle to realization. Inasmuch as the effulgence is one effulgence, the human realities must all become recipients of the same light, recognizing in it the compelling force that unites them in its illumination.

As this is the radiant century, it is my hope that the Sun of Truth may illumine all humanity. May the eyes be opened and the ears become attentive; may souls become resuscitated and consort together in the utmost harmony as recipients of the same light. Perchance, God will remove this strife and warfare of thousands of years. May this bloodshed pass away, this

tyranny and oppression cease, this warfare be ended.
May the light of love shine forth and illumine hearts,
and may human lives be cemented and connected
until all of us may find agreement and tranquillity
beneath the same tabernacle and with the standard of
the Most Great Peace above us move steadily onward.

O Thou kind Lord! O Thou Who art generous
and merciful! We are the servants of Thy threshold
and are gathered beneath the sheltering shadow of
Thy divine unity. The sun of Thy mercy is shining
upon all, and the clouds of Thy bounty shower upon
all. Thy gifts encompass all, Thy loving providence
sustains all, Thy protection overshadows all, and the
glances of Thy favor are cast upon all. O Lord! Grant
Thine infinite bestowals, and let the light of Thy
guidance shine. Illumine the eyes, gladden the hearts
with abiding joy. Confer a new spirit upon all people
and bestow upon them eternal life. Unlock the gates
of true understanding and let the light of faith shine
resplendent. Gather all people beneath the shadow of
Thy bounty and cause them to unite in harmony, so
that they may become as the rays of one sun, as the
waves of one ocean, and as the fruit of one tree. May
they drink from the same fountain. May they be refreshed by the same breeze. May they receive illumination from the same source of light. Thou art the
Giver, the Merciful, the Omnipotent.

TALK AT RECEPTION AT METROPOLITAN TEMPLE

Seventh Avenue and Fourteenth Street
New York

Notes by Esther Foster

The Fatherhood of God, His loving-kindness and beneficence are apparent to all. In His mercy He provides fully and amply for His creatures, and if any soul sins, He does not suspend His bounty. All created things are visible manifestations of His Fatherhood, mercy and heavenly bestowals. Human brotherhood is, likewise, as clear and evident as the sun, for all are servants of one God, belong to one humankind, inhabit the same globe, are sheltered beneath the overshadowing dome of heaven and submerged in the sea of divine mercy. Human brotherhood and dependence exist because mutual helpfulness and cooperation are the two necessary principles underlying human welfare. This is the physical relationship of mankind. There is another brotherhood—the spiritual—which is higher, holier and superior to all others. It is heavenly; it emanates from the breaths of the Holy Spirit and the effulgence of merciful attributes; it is founded upon spiritual susceptibilities. This brotherhood is established by the Manifestations of the Holy One.

The divine Manifestations since the day of Adam have striven to unite humanity so that all may be accounted as one soul. The function and purpose of a shepherd is to gather and not disperse his flock. The Prophets of God have been divine Shepherds of humanity. They have established a bond of love and unity among mankind, made scattered peoples one nation and wandering tribes a mighty kingdom. They have laid the foundation of the oneness of God and summoned all to universal peace. All these holy, divine Manifestations are one. They have served one God, promulgated the same truth, founded the same institutions and reflected the same light. Their appearances have been successive and correlated; each One has announced and extolled the One Who was to follow, and all laid the foundation of reality. They summoned and invited the people to love and made the human world a mirror of the Word of God. Therefore, the divine religions They established have one foundation; Their teachings, proofs and evidences are one; in name and form They differ, but in reality They agree and are the same. These holy Manifestations have been as the coming of springtime in the world. Although the springtime of this year is designated by another name according to the changing calendar, yet as regards its life and quickening it is the same as the springtime of last year. For each spring is the time of a new creation, the effects, bestowals, perfections and life-giving forces of which are the same as those of the former vernal seasons, although the names are many and various. This is 1912, last year was 1911 and so on, but in fundamental reality no difference is apparent. The sun is one, but the dawning points of the sun are numerous and changing. The ocean is one body of water, but different parts of it have particular designations—Atlantic, Pacific, Mediterranean, Antarctic, etc. If we consider the names, there is differentiation; but the water, the ocean itself, is one reality.

Likewise, the divine religions of the holy Manifestations of God are in reality one, though in name and nomenclature they differ. Man must be a lover of the light, no matter from what dayspring it may appear. He must be a lover of the rose, no matter in what soil it may be growing. He must be a seeker of the truth, no matter from what source it come. Attachment to the lantern is not loving the light. Attachment to the earth is not befitting, but enjoyment of the rose which develops from the soil is worthy. Devotion to the tree is profitless, but partaking of the fruit is beneficial. Luscious fruits, no matter upon what tree they grow or where they may be found, must be enjoyed. The word of truth, no matter which tongue utters it, must be sanctioned. Absolute verities, no matter in what book they be recorded, must be accepted. If we harbor prejudice, it will be the cause of deprivation and ignorance. The strife between religions, nations and races arises from misunderstanding. If we investigate the religions to discover the principles underlying their foundations, we will find they agree; for the fundamental reality of them is one and not multiple. By this means the religionists of the world will reach their point of unity and reconciliation. They will ascertain the truth that the purpose of religion is the acquisition of praiseworthy virtues, the betterment of morals, the spiritual development of mankind, the real life and divine bestowals. All the Prophets have been the promoters of these principles; none of Them has been the promoter of corruption, vice or evil. They have summoned mankind to all good. They have united people in the love of God, invited them to the religions of the unity of mankind and exhorted them to amity and agreement. For example, we mention Abraham and Moses. By this mention we do not mean the limitation implied in the mere names but intend the virtues which these names embody. When we say Abraham, we mean thereby a manifestation of divine guidance, a center of human virtues, a source of heavenly bestowals to mankind, a dawning point of divine inspiration and perfections. These perfections and graces are not limited to names and boundaries. When we find these virtues, qualities and attributes in any personality, we recognize the same reality shining from within and bow in acknowledgment of the Abrahamic perfections. Similarly, we acknowledge and adore the beauty of Moses. Some souls were lovers of the name Abraham, loving the lantern instead of the light, and when they saw this same light shining from another lantern, they were so attached to the former lantern that they did not recognize its later appearance and illumination. Therefore, those who were attached and held tenaciously to the name Abraham were deprived when the Abrahamic virtues reappeared in Moses. Similarly, the Jews were believers in Moses, awaiting the coming of the Messiah. The virtues and perfections of Moses became apparent in Jesus Christ most effulgently, but the Jews held to the name Moses, not adoring the virtues and perfections manifest in Him. Had they been adoring these virtues and seeking these perfections, they would assuredly have believed in Jesus Christ when the same virtues and perfections shone in Him. If we are lovers of the light, we adore it in whatever lamp it may become manifest, but if we love the lamp itself and the light is transferred to another lamp, we will neither accept nor sanction it. Therefore, we must follow and adore the virtues revealed in the Messengers of God—whether in Abraham, Moses, Jesus or other Prophets—but we must not adhere to and adore the lamp. We must recognize the sun, no matter from what dawning point it may shine forth, be it Mosaic, Abrahamic or any personal point of orientation whatever, for we are lovers of sunlight and not of orientation. We are lovers of illumination and not of lamps and candles. We are seekers for water, no matter from what rock it may gush forth. We are in need of fruit in whatsoever orchard it may be ripened. We long for rain; it matters not which cloud pours it down. We must not be fettered. If we renounce these fetters, we shall agree, for all are seekers of reality. The counterfeit or imitation of true religion has adulterated human belief, and the foundations have been lost sight of. The variance of these imitations has produced enmity and strife, war and bloodshed. Now the glorious and brilliant twentieth century has dawned, and the divine bounty is radiating universally. The Sun of Truth is shining forth in intense enkindlement. This is, verily, the century when these imitations must be forsaken, superstitions abandoned and God alone worshiped. We must look at the reality of the Prophets and Their teachings in order that we may agree.

Praise be to God! The springtime of God is at hand. This century is, verily, the spring season. The world of mind and kingdom of soul have become fresh and verdant by its bestowals. It has resuscitated the whole realm of existence. On one hand, the lights of reality are shining; on the other, the clouds of divine mercy are pouring down the fullness of heavenly bounty. Wonderful material progress is evident, and great spiritual discoveries are being made. Truly, this can be called the miracle of centuries, for it is replete with manifestations of the miraculous. The time has come when all mankind shall be united, when all races shall be loyal to one fatherland, all religions become one religion, and racial and religious bias pass away. It is a day in which the oneness of humankind shall uplift its standard and international peace, like the true morning, flood the world with its light. Therefore, we offer supplications to God, asking Him to dispel these gloomy clouds and uproot these imitations in order that the East and West may become radiant with love and unity, that the nations of the world shall embrace each other and the ideal spiritual brotherhood illumine the world like the glorious sun of the high heavens. This is our hope, our wish and desire. We pray that through the bounty and grace of God we may attain thereto. I am very happy to be present at this meeting which has innate radiance, intelligence, perception and longing to investigate reality. Such meetings are the glory of the world of mankind. I ask the blessing of God in your behalf.

16 June 1912

_____

TALK AT
CENTRAL
CONGREGATIONAL
CHURCH

_____

Hancock Street
Brooklyn, New York

Notes by Esther Foster

This is a goodly temple and congregation, for—praise be to God!—this is a house of worship wherein conscientious opinion has free sway. Every religion and every religious aspiration may be freely voiced and expressed here. Just as in the world of politics there is need for free thought, likewise in the world of religion there should be the right of unrestricted individual belief. Consider what a vast difference exists between modern democracy and the old forms of despotism. Under an autocratic government the opinions of men are not free, and development is stifled, whereas in democracy, because thought and speech are not restricted, the greatest progress is witnessed. It is likewise true in the world of religion. When freedom of conscience, liberty of thought and right of speech prevail—that is to say, when every man according to his own idealization may give expression to his beliefs—development and growth are inevitable. Therefore, this is a blessed church because its pulpit is open to every religion, the ideals of which may be set forth with openness and freedom. For this reason I am most grateful to the reverend doctor; I find him indeed a servant of the oneness of humanity.

The holy Manifestations Who have been the Sources or Founders of the various religious systems were united and agreed in purpose and teaching. Abraham, Moses, Zoroaster, Buddha, Jesus, Muḥammad, the Báb and Bahá'u'lláh are one in spirit and reality. Moreover, each Prophet fulfilled the promise of the One Who came before Him and, likewise, Each announced the One Who would follow. Consider how Abraham foretold the coming of Moses, and Moses embodied the Abrahamic statement. Moses prophesied the Messianic cycle, and Christ fulfilled the law of Moses. It is evident, therefore, that the Holy Manifestations Who founded the religious systems are united and agreed; there is no differentiation possible in Their mission and teachings; all are reflectors of reality, and all are promulgators of the religion of God. The divine religion is reality, and reality is not multiple; it is one. Therefore, the foundations of the religious systems are one because all proceed from the indivisible reality; but the followers of these systems have disagreed; discord, strife and warfare have arisen among them, for they have forsaken the foundation and held to that which is but imitation and semblance. Inasmuch as imitations differ, enmity and dissension have resulted. For example, Jesus Christ—may my spirit be a sacrifice unto Him!—laid the foundation of eternal reality, but after His departure many sects and divisions appeared in Christianity. What was the cause of this? There is no doubt that they originated in dogmatic imitations, for the foundations of Christ were reality itself, in which no divergence exists. When imitations appeared, sects and denominations were formed.

If Christians of all denominations and divisions should investigate reality, the foundations of Christ will unite them. No enmity or hatred will remain, for they will all be under the one guidance of reality itself. Likewise, in the wider field if all the existing religious systems will turn away from ancestral imitations and investigate reality, seeking the real meanings of the Holy Books, they will unite and agree upon the same foundation, reality itself. As long as they follow counterfeit doctrines or imitations instead of reality, animosity and discord will exist and increase. Let me illustrate this. Moses and the prophets of Israel announced the advent of the Messiah but expressed it in the language of symbols. When Christ appeared, the Jews rejected Him, although they were expecting His manifestation and in their temples and synagogues were crying and lamenting, saying, "O God, hasten the coming of the Messiah!" Why did they deny Him when He announced Himself? Because they had followed ancestral forms and interpretations and were blind to the reality of Christ. They had not perceived the inner significances of the Holy Bible. They voiced their objections, saying, "We are expecting Christ, but His coming is conditioned upon certain fulfillments and prophetic announcements. Among the signs of His appearance is one that He shall come from an unknown place, whereas now this claimant of Messiahship has come from Nazareth. We know his home, and we are acquainted with his mother.

"Second, one of the signs or Messianic conditions is that His scepter would be an iron rod, and this Christ has not even a wooden staff.

"Third, He was to be seated upon the throne of David, whereas this Messianic king is in the utmost state of poverty and has not even a mat.

"Fourth, He was to conquer the East and the West. This person has not even conquered a village. How can he be the Messiah?

"Fifth, He was to promulgate the laws of the Bible. This one has not only failed to promulgate the laws of the Bible, but he has broken the law of the sabbath.

"Sixth, the Messiah was to gather together all the Jews who were scattered in Palestine and restore them to honor and prestige, but this one has degraded the Jews instead of uplifting them.

"Seventh, during His sovereignty even the animals were to enjoy blessings and comfort, for according to the prophetic texts, He should establish peace to such a universal extent that the eagle and quail would live together, the lion and deer would feed in the same meadow, the wolf and lamb would lie down in the same pasture. In the human kingdom warfare was to cease entirely; spears would be turned into pruning hooks and swords into plowshares. Now we see in the day of this would-be Messiah such injustice prevails that even he himself is sacrificed. How could he be the promised Christ?"

And so they spoke infamous words regarding Him.

Now inasmuch as the Jews were submerged in the sea of ancestral imitations, they could not comprehend the meaning of these prophecies. All the words of the prophets were fulfilled, but because the Jews held tenaciously to hereditary interpretations, they did not understand the inner meanings of the Holy Bible; therefore, they denied Jesus Christ, the Messiah. The purpose of the prophetic words was not the outward or literal meaning, but the inner symbolical significance. For example, it was announced that the Messiah was to come from an unknown place. This did not refer to the birthplace of the physical body of Jesus. It has reference to the reality of the Christ— that is to say, the Christ reality was to appear from the invisible realm—for the divine reality of Christ is holy and sanctified above place.

His sword was to be a sword of iron. This signified His tongue which should separate the true from the false and by which great sword of attack He would conquer the kingdoms of hearts. He did not conquer by the physical power of an iron rod; He conquered the East and the West by the sword of His utterance.

He was seated upon the throne of David, but His sovereignty was neither a Napoleonic sovereignty nor the vanishing dominion of a Pharaoh. The Christ Kingdom was everlasting, eternal in the heaven of the divine Will.

By His promulgating the laws of the Bible the reality of the law of Moses was meant. The Sinaitic law is the foundation of the reality of Christianity. Christ promulgated it and gave it higher, spiritual expression.

He conquered and subdued the East and West. His conquest was effected through the breaths of the Holy Spirit, which eliminated all boundaries and shone from all horizons.

In His day, according to prophecy, the wolf and the lamb were to drink from the same fountain. This was realized in Christ. The fountain referred to was the Gospel, from which the water of life gushes forth. The wolf and lamb are opposed and divergent races symbolized by these animals. Their meeting and association were impossible, but having become believers in Jesus Christ those who were formerly as wolves and lambs became united through the words of the Gospel.

The purport is that all the meanings of the prophecies were fulfilled, but because the Jews were captives of ancestral imitations and did not perceive the reality of the meanings of these words, they denied Christ; nay, they even went so far as to crucify Him. Consider how harmful is imitation. These were interpretations handed down from fathers and ancestors, and because the Jews held fast to them, they were deprived.

It is evident, then, that we must forsake all such imitations and beliefs so that we may not commit this error. We must investigate reality, lay aside selfish notions and banish hearsay from our minds. The Jews consider Christ the enemy of Moses, whereas, on the contrary, Christ promoted the Word of Moses. He spread the name of Moses throughout the Orient and

Occident. He promulgated the teachings of Moses. Had it not been for Christ, you would not have heard the name of Moses; and unless the manifestation of Messiahship had appeared in Christ, we would not have received the Old Testament.

The truth is that Christ fulfilled the Mosaic law and in every way upheld Moses; but the Jews, blinded by imitations and prejudices, considered Him the enemy of Moses.

Among the great religious systems of the world is Islám. About three hundred million people acknowledge it. For more than a thousand years there has been enmity and strife between Muslims and Christians, owing to misunderstanding and spiritual blindness. If prejudices and imitations were abandoned, there would be no enmity whatever between them, and these hundreds of millions of antagonistic religionists would adorn the world of humanity by their unity.

I wish now to call your attention to a most important point. All Islám considers the Qur'án the Word of God. In this sacred Book there are explicit texts which are not traditional, stating that Christ was the Word of God, that He was the Spirit of God, that Jesus Christ came into this world through the quickening breaths of the Holy Spirit and that Mary, His mother, was holy and sanctified. In the Qur'án a whole chapter is devoted to the story of Jesus. It records that in the time of His youth He worshiped God in the temple at Jerusalem, that manna descended from heaven for His sustenance and that He uttered words immediately after His birth. In brief, in the Qur'án there is eulogy and commendation of Christ such as you do not find in the Gospel. The Gospel does not record that the child Jesus spoke at birth or that God caused sustenance to descend from heaven for Him, but in the Qur'án it is repeatedly stated that God sent down manna day by day as food for Him. Furthermore, it is significant and convincing that when Muḥammad proclaimed His work and mission, His first objection to His own followers was, "Why have you not believed on Jesus Christ? Why have you not accepted the Gospel? Why have you not believed in Moses? Why have you not followed the precepts of the Old Testament? Why have you not understood the prophets of Israel? Why have you not believed in the disciples of Christ? The first duty incumbent upon ye, O Arabians, is to accept and believe in these. You must consider Moses as a Prophet. You must accept Jesus Christ as the Word of God. You must know the Old and the New Testaments as the Word of God. You must believe in Jesus Christ as the product of the Holy Spirit." His people answered, "O Muḥammad! We will become believers although our fathers and ancestors were not believers, and we are proud of them. Tell us what is going to become of them?" Muḥammad replied, "I declare unto you that they occupy the lowest stratum of hell because they did not believe in Moses and Christ and because they did not accept the Bible; and although they are my own ancestors, yet they are in despair in hell." This is an explicit text of the Qur'án; it is not a story or tradition but from the Qur'án itself, which is in the hands of the people. Therefore, it is evident that ignorance and misunderstanding have caused so much warfare and strife between Christians and Muslims. If both should investigate the underlying truth of their religious beliefs, the outcome would be unity and agreement; strife and bitterness would pass away forever and the world of humanity find peace and composure. Consider that there are two hundred and fifty million Christians and three hundred million Muslims. How much blood has flowed in their wars; how many nations have been destroyed; how many children have been made fatherless; how many fathers and mothers have mourned the loss of children and dear ones! All this has been due to prejudice, misunderstanding and imitations of ancestral beliefs without investigation of reality. If the Holy Books were rightly understood, none of this discord and distress would have existed, but love and fellowship would have prevailed instead. This is true with all the other religions as well. The conditions I have named will apply equally to all. The essential purpose of the religion of God is to establish unity among mankind. The divine Manifestations were Founders of the means of fellowship and love. They did not come to create discord, strife and hatred in the world. The religion of God is the cause of love, but if it is made to be the source of enmity and bloodshed, surely its absence is preferable to its existence; for then it becomes satanic, detrimental and an obstacle to the human world.

In the Orient the various peoples and nations were in a state of antagonism and strife, manifesting the utmost enmity and hatred toward each other. Darkness encompassed the world of mankind. At such a time as this Bahá'u'lláh appeared. He removed all the imitations and prejudices which had caused separation and misunderstanding and laid the foundation of the one religion of God. When this was accomplished, Muslims, Christians, Jews, Zoroastrians, Buddhists all were united in actual fellowship and love. The souls who followed Bahá'u'lláh from every natio have become as one family living in agreement and accord, willing to sacrifice life for each other. The Muslim will give his life for the Christian, the Christian for the Jew and all of them for the Zoroastrian. They live together in love, fellowship and unity. They have attained to the condition of rebirth in the Spirit of God. They have become revivified and regenerated through the breaths of the Holy Spirit. Praise be to God! This light has come forth from the East, and eventually there shall be no discord or enmity in the Orient. Through the power of Bahá'u'lláh all will be united. He upraised this standard of the oneness of humanity in prison. When subjected to banishment by two kings, while a refugee from enemies of all nations and during the days of His long imprisonment He wrote to the kings and rulers of the world in words of wonderful eloquence, arraigning them severely and summoning them to the divine standard of unity and justice. He exhorted them to peace and international agreement, making it incumbent upon them to establish a board of international arbitration—that from all nations and governments of the world there should be delegates selected for a congress of nations which should constitute a universal arbitral court of justice to settle international disputes. He wrote to Victoria, Queen of Great Britain, the Czar of Russia, the Emperor of Germany, Napoleon III of France and others, inviting them to world unity and peace. Through a heavenly power He was enabled to promulgate these ideals in the Orient. Kings could not withstand Him. They endeavored to extinguish His light but served only to increase its intensity and illumination. While in prison He stood against the S͟háh of Persia and Sulṭán of Turkey and promulgated His teachings until He firmly established the banner of truth and the oneness of humankind. I was a prisoner with Him for forty years until the Young Turks of the Committee of Union and Progress overthrew the despotism of ʿAbdu'l-Ḥamíd, dethroned him and proclaimed liberty. This committee set me free from tyranny and oppression; otherwise, I should have been in prison until the days of my life were ended. The purport is this: that Bahá'u'lláh in prison was able to proclaim and establish the foundations of peace although two despotic kings were His enemies and oppressors. The King of Persia, Náṣiri'd-Dín S͟háh, had killed twenty thousand Bahá'ís, martyrs who in absolute severance and complete willingness offered their lives joyfully for their faith. These two powerful and tyrannical kings could not withstand a prisoner; this Prisoner upheld the standard of humanity and brought the people of the Orient into agreement and unity. Today in the East, only those who have not followed Bahá'u'lláh are in opposition and enmity. The people of the nations who have accepted Him as the standard of divine guidance enjoy a condition of actual fellowship and love. If you should attend a meeting in the East, you could not distinguish between Christian and Muslim; you would not know which was Jew, Zoroastrian or Buddhist, so completely have they become fraternized and their religious differences been leveled. They associate in the utmost love and spiritual fragrance as if they belonged to one family, as if they were one people.

17 August 1912

———————————

TALK AT
GREEN ACRE

———————————

Eliot, Maine

Notes by Edna McKinney

The physical beauty of this place is very wonderful. We hope that a spiritual charm may surround and halo it; then its beauty will be perfect. There is a spiritual atmosphere manifest here particularly at sunset.

In cities like New York the people are submerged in the sea of materialism. Their sensibilities are attuned to material forces, their perceptions purely physical. The animal energies predominate in their activities; all their thoughts are directed to material things; day and night they are devoted to the attractions of this world, without aspiration beyond the life that is vanishing and mortal. In schools and temples of learning knowledge of the sciences acquired is based upon material observations only; there is no realization of Divinity in their methods and conclusions—all have reference to the world of matter. They are not interested in attaining knowledge of the mysteries of God or understanding the secrets of the heavenly Kingdom; what they acquire is based altogether upon visible and tangible evidences. Beyond these evidences they are without susceptibilities; they have no idea of the world of inner significances and are utterly out of touch with God, considering this an indication of reasonable attitude and philosophical judgment whereof they are self-sufficient and proud.

As a matter of fact, this supposed excellence is possessed in its superlative degree by the animals. The animals are without knowledge of God; so to speak, they are deniers of Divinity and understand nothing of the Kingdom and its heavenly mysteries. As deniers of the Kingdom, they are utterly ignorant of spiritual things and uninformed of the supernatural world. Therefore, if it be a perfection and virtue to be without knowledge of God and His Kingdom, the animals have attained the highest degree of excellence and proficiency. Then the donkey is the greatest scientist and the cow an accomplished naturalist, for they have obtained what they know without schooling and years of laborious study in colleges, trusting implicitly to the evidence of the senses and relying solely upon intuitive virtues. The cow, for instance, is a lover of the visible and a believer in the tangible, contented and happy when pasture is plenty, perfectly serene, a blissful exponent of the transcendental school of philosophy. Such is the status of the material philosophers, who glory in sharing the condition of the cow, imagining themselves in a lofty station. Reflect upon their ignorance and blindness.

Nay, rather, the virtue of man is this: that he can investigate the ideals of the Kingdom and attain knowledge which is denied the animal in its limitation. The station of man is this: that he has the power to attain those ideals and thereby differentiate and consciously distinguish himself an infinite degree above the kingdoms of existence below him.

The station of man is great, very great. God has created man after His own image and likeness. He has endowed him with a mighty power which is capable of discovering the mysteries of phenomena. Through its use man is able to arrive at ideal conclusions instead of being restricted to the mere plane of sense impressions. As he possesses sense endowment in common with the animals, it is evident that he is distinguished above them by his conscious power of penetrating abstract realities. He acquires divine wisdom; he searches out the mysteries of creation; he witnesses the radiance of omnipotence; he attains the second birth— that is to say, he is born out of the material world just as he is born of the mother; he attains to everlasting life; he draws nearer to God; his heart is replete with the love of God. This is the foundation of the world of humanity; this is the image and likeness of God; this is the reality of man; otherwise, he is an animal. Verily, God has created the animal in the image and likeness of man, for though man outwardly is human, yet in nature he possesses animal tendencies.

You must endeavor to understand the mysteries of God, attain the ideal knowledge and arrive at the station of vision, acquiring directly from the Sun of Reality and receiving a destined portion from the ancient bestowal of God.

6 November 1912

TALK AT UNIVERSALIST CHURCH

Thirteenth and L Streets, NW
Washington, D.C.

Notes by Joseph H. Hannen

Praise be to God! The standard of liberty is held aloft in this land. You enjoy political liberty; you enjoy liberty of thought and speech, religious liberty, racial and personal liberty. Surely this is worthy of appreciation and thanksgiving. In this connection let me mention the freedom, hospitality and universal welcome extended to me during my recent travels throughout America. I wish also to reciprocate fully and completely the warm greeting and friendly attitude of the reverend doctor, pastor of this church, whose loving and quickened susceptibilities especially command acknowledgment. Surely men who are leaders of thought must conform to the example of his kindliness and goodwill. Liberalism is essential in this day—justness and equity toward all nations and people. Human attitudes must not be limited; for God is unlimited, and whosoever is the servant of the threshold of God must, likewise, be free from limitations. The world of existence is an emanation of the merciful attribute of God. God has shone forth upon the phenomena of being through His effulgence of mercy, and He is clement and kind to all His creation. Therefore, the world of humanity must ever be the recipient of bounties from His majesty, the eternal Lord, even as Christ has declared, "Be ye therefore perfect, even as your Father which is in heaven is perfect." For His bounties, like the light and heat of the sun in the material heavens, descend alike upon all mankind. Consequently, man must learn the lesson of kindness and beneficence from God Himself. Just as God is kind to all humanity, man also must be kind to his fellow creatures. If his attitude is just and loving toward his fellowmen, toward all creation, then indeed is he worthy of being pronounced the image and likeness of God.

Brotherhood, or fraternity, is of different kinds. It may be family association, the intimate relationship of the household. This is limited and subject to change and disruption. How often it happens that in a family love and agreement are changed into enmity and antagonism. Another form of fraternity is manifest in patriotism. Man loves his fellowmen because they belong to the same native land. This is also limited and subject to change and disintegration as, for instance, when sons of the same fatherland are opposed to each other in war, bloodshed and battle. Still another brotherhood, or fraternity, is that which arises from racial unity, the oneness of racial origin, producing ties of affinity and association. This, likewise, has its limitation and liability to change, for often war and deadly strife have been witnessed between people and nations of the same racial lineage. There is a fourth kind of brotherhood, the attitude of man toward humanity itself, the altruistic love of humankind and recognition of the fundamental human bond. Although this is unlimited, it is, nevertheless, susceptible to change and destruction. Even from this universal fraternal bond the looked-for result does not appear. What is the looked-for result? Loving-kindness among all human creatures and a firm, inde-structible brotherhood which includes all the divine possibilities and significances in humanity. Therefore, it is evident that fraternity, love and kindness based upon family, native land, race or an attitude of al-truism are neither sufficient nor permanent since all of them are limited, restricted and liable to change and disruption. For in the family there is discord and alienation; among sons of the same fatherland, strife and internecine warfare are witnessed; between those of a given race, hostility and hatred are frequent; and even among the altruists, varying aspects of opinion and lack of unselfish devotion give little promise of permanent and indestructible unity among mankind.

Therefore, the Lord of mankind has caused His holy, divine Manifestations to come into the world. He has revealed His heavenly Books in order to es-tablish spiritual brotherhood and through the power of the Holy Spirit has made it practicable for perfect fraternity to be realized among mankind. And when through the breaths of the Holy Spirit this perfect fra-ternity and agreement are established amongst men— this brotherhood and love being spiritual in character, this loving-kindness being heavenly, these constraining bonds being divine—a unity appears which is indissoluble, unchanging and never subject to transformation. It is ever the same and will forever remain the same. For example, consider the foundation of the brotherhood laid by Christ. Observe how that fraternity was conducive to unity and accord and how it brought various souls to a plane of uniform attainment where they were willing to sacrifice their lives for each other. They were content to renounce possessions and ready to forfeit joyously life itself. They lived together in such love and fellowship that even Galen, the famous Greek philosopher who was not a Christian, in his work entitled "The Progress of the Nations" said that religious beliefs are greatly conducive to the foundation of real civilization. As a proof thereof he said, "A certain number of people contemporaneous with us are known as Christians. These enjoy the superlative degree of moral civilization. Each one of them is as a great philosopher because they live together in the utmost love and good fellowship. They sacrifice life for each other. They offer worldly possessions for each other. You can say of the Christian people that they are as one person. There is a bond amongst them that is indissoluble in character."

It is evident, therefore, that the foundation of real brotherhood, the cause of loving cooperation and reciprocity and the source of real kindness and unselfish devotion is none other than the breaths of the Holy Spirit. Without this influence and animus it is impossible. We may be able to realize some degrees of fraternity through other motives, but these are limited associations and subject to change. When human brotherhood is founded upon the Holy Spirit, it is eternal, changeless, unlimited.

In various parts of the Orient there was a time when brotherhood, loving-kindness and all the praiseworthy qualities of mankind seemed to have disappeared. There was no evidence of patriotic, religious or racial fraternity; but conditions of bigotry, hatred and prejudice prevailed instead. The adherents of each religion were violent enemies of the others, filled with the spirit of hostility and eager for shedding of blood. The present war in the Balkans furnishes a parallel of these conditions. Consider the bloodshed, ferocity and oppression manifested there even in this enlightened century—all of it based fundamentally upon religious prejudice and disagreement. For the nations involved belong to the same races and native lands; nevertheless, they are savage and merciless toward each other. Similar deplorable conditions prevailed in Persia in the nineteenth century. Darkness and ignorant fanaticism were widespread; no trace of fellowship or brotherhood existed amongst the races. On the contrary, human hearts were filled with rage and hatred; darkness and gloom were manifest in human lives and conditions everywhere. At such a time as this Bahá'u'lláh appeared upon the divine horizon, even as the glory of the sun, and in that gross darkness and hopelessness of the human world there shone a great light. He founded the oneness of the world of humanity, declaring that all mankind are as sheep and that God is the real and true Shepherd. The Shepherd is one, and all people are of His flock.

The world of humanity is one, and God is equally kind to all. What, then, is the source of unkindness and hatred in the human world? This real Shepherd loves all His sheep. He leads them in green pastures. He rears and protects them. What, then, is the source of enmity and alienation among humankind? Whence this conflict and strife? The real underlying cause is lack of religious unity and association, for in each of the great religions we find superstition, blind imitation of creeds, and theological formulas adhered to instead of the divine fundamentals, causing difference and divergence among mankind instead of agreement and fellowship. Consequently, strife, hatred and warfare have arisen, based upon this divergence and separation. If we investigate the foundations of the divine religions, we find them to be one, absolutely changeless and never subject to transformation. For example, each of the divine religions contains two kinds of laws or ordinances. One division concerns the world of morality and ethical institutions. These are the essential ordinances. They instill and awaken the knowledge and love of God, love for humanity, the virtues of the world of mankind, the attributes of the divine Kingdom, rebirth and resurrection from the kingdom of nature. These constitute one kind of divine law which is common to all and never subject to change. From the dawn of the Adamic cycle to the present day this fundamental law of God has continued changeless. This is the foundation of divine religion.

The second division comprises laws and institutions which provide for human needs and conditions according to exigencies of time and place. These are accidental, of no essential importance and should never have been made the cause and source of human contention. For example, during the time of Moses—upon Him be peace!—according to the exigencies of that period, divorce was permissible. During the cycle of Christ, inasmuch as divorce was not in conformity with the time and conditions, Jesus Christ abrogated it. In the cycle of Moses plurality of wives was permissible. But during the time of Christ the exigency which had sanctioned it did not exist; therefore, it was forbidden. Moses lived in the wilderness and desert of Sinai; therefore, His ordinances and commandments were in conformity with those conditions. The penalty for theft was to cut off a man's hand. An ordinance of this kind was in keeping with desert life but is not compatible with conditions of the present day. Such ordinances, therefore, constitute the second or nonessential division of the divine religions and are not of importance, for they deal with human transactions which are ever changing according to the requirements of time and place.

Therefore, the intrinsic foundations of the divine religions are one. As this is true, why should hostility and strife exist among them? Why should this hatred and warfare, ferocity and bloodshed continue? Is this allowable and justified? God forbid!

An essential principle of Bahá'u'lláh's teaching is that religion must be the cause of unity and love amongst men; that it is the supreme effulgence of Divinity, the stimulus of life, the source of honor and productive of eternal existence. Religion is not intended to arouse enmity and hatred nor to become the source of tyranny and injustice. Should it prove to be the cause of hostility, discord and the alienation of mankind, assuredly the absence of religion would be preferable. Religious teachings are like a course of treatment having for its purpose the cure and healing of mankind. If the only outcome of a course of treatment should be mere diagnosis and fruitless discussion of symptoms, it would be better to abandon and abolish it. In this sense the absence of religion would be at least some progress toward unity.

Furthermore, religion must conform to reason and be in accord with the conclusions of science. For religion, reason and science are realities; therefore, these three, being realities, must conform and be reconciled. A question or principle which is religious in its nature must be sanctioned by science. Science must declare it to be valid, and reason must confirm it in order that it may inspire confidence. If religious teaching, however, be at variance with science and reason, it is unquestionably superstition. The Lord of mankind has bestowed upon us the faculty of reason whereby we may discern the realities of things. How then can man rightfully accept any proposition which is not in conformity with the processes of reason and the principles of science? Assuredly such a course cannot inspire man with confidence and real belief.

The teachings of Bahá'u'lláh embody many principles; I am giving you only a synopsis. One of these principles concerns equality between men and women. He declared that as all are created in the image and likeness of the one God, there is no distinction as to sex in the estimation of God. He who is purest in heart, whose knowledge exceeds and who excels in kindness to the servants of God, is nearest and dearest to the Lord, our Creator, irrespective of sex. In the lower kingdoms, the animal and vegetable, we find sex differentiation in function and organism. All plants, trees and animals are subject to that differentiation by creation, but among themselves there is absolute equality without further distinction as to sex. Why, then, should mankind make a distinction which the lower creatures do not regard? Especially so when we realize that all are of the same kingdom and kindred; that all are the leaves of one tree, the waves of one sea? The only reasonable explanation is that woman has not been afforded the same educational facilities as man. For if she had received the same opportunities for training and development as man has enjoyed, undoubtedly she would have attained the same station and level. In the estimate of God no distinction exists; both are as one and possess equal degrees of capacity. Therefore, through opportunity and development woman will merit and attain the same prerogatives. When Jesus Christ died upon the cross, the disciples who witnessed His crucifixion were disturbed and shaken. Even Peter, one of the greatest of His followers, denied Him thrice. Mary Magdalene brought them together and confirmed their faith, saying, "Why are ye doubting? Why have ye feared? O thou Peter! Why didst thou deny Him? For Christ was not crucified. The reality of Christ is ever-living, everlasting, eternal. For that divine reality there is no beginning, no ending, and, therefore, there can be no death. At most, only the body of Jesus has suffered death." In brief, this woman, singly and alone, was instrumental in transforming the disciples and making them steadfast. This is an evidence of extraordinary power and supreme attributes, a proof that woman is the equivalent and complement of man. The one who is better trained and educated, whose aptitude is greater and whose ideals are higher is most distinguished and worthy—whether man or woman.

Through the teachings of Bahá'u'lláh the horizon of the East was made radiant and glorious. Souls who have hearkened to His words and accepted His message live together today in complete fellowship and love. They even offer their lives for each other. They forego and renounce worldly possessions for one another, each preferring the other to himself. This has

been due to the declaration and foundation of the oneness of the world of humanity. Today in Persia there
are meetings and assemblages wherein souls who have
become illumined by the teachings of Bahá'u'lláh—
representative Muslims, Christians, Jews, Zoroastrians, Buddhists and of the various denominations of
each—mingle and conjoin in perfect fellowship and
absolute agreement. A wonderful brotherhood and
love is established among them, and all are united in
spirit and service for international peace. More than
twenty thousand Bahá'ís have given their lives in mar-
tyrdom for the Cause of God. The governments of
the East arose against them, bent upon their extermi-
nation. They were killed relentlessly, but day by day
their numbers have increased, day by day they have
multiplied in strength and become more eloquent.
They have been strengthened through the efficacy of
a wonderful spiritual power. How savage and fearful
the ferocity of man against his fellowman! Consider
what is taking place now in the Balkans, what blood is
being shed. Even the wild beasts and ferocious animals
do not commit such acts. The most ferocious wolf
kills but one sheep a day, and even that for his food.
But now in the Balkans one man destroys ten fellow
beings. The commanders of armies glory in having
killed ten thousand men, not for food, nay, rather, for
military control, territorial greed, fame and possession
of the dust of the earth. They kill for national aggrandizement, notwithstanding this terrestrial globe is but
a dark world of grossest matter. It is a world of sorrow

and grief, a world of disappointment and unhappiness, a world of death. For after all, the earth is but the everlasting graveyard, the vast, universal cemetery of all mankind. Yet men fight to possess this graveyard, waging war and battle, killing each other. What ignorance! How spacious the earth is with room in plenty for all! How thoughtful the providence which has so allotted that every man may derive his sustenance from it! The Lord, our Creator, does not ordain that anyone should starve or live in want. All are intended to participate in the blessed and abundant bestowals of our God. Fundamentally, all warfare and bloodshed in the human world are due to the lack of unity between the religions, which through superstitions and adherence to theological dogmas have obscured the one reality which is the source and basis of them all.

As to the American people: This noble nation, intelligent, thoughtful, reflective, is not impelled by motives of territorial aggrandizement and lust for dominion. Its boundaries are insular and geographically separated from the other nations. Here we find a oneness of interest and unity of national policy. These are, indeed, United States. Therefore, this nation possesses the capacity and capability for holding aloft the banner of international peace. May this noble people be the cause of unifying humanity. May they spread broadcast the heavenly civilization and illumination, become the cause of the diffusion of the love of God, proclaim the solidarity of mankind and be the cause of the guidance of the human race. Therefore, I ask that you will give this all-important question your most serious consideration and efforts. May the world of humanity find peace and composure and this dark earth be transformed into a realm of radiance. May the East and West clasp hands together. May the oneness of God become reflected and fully revealed in the hearts of humanity and all mankind prove to be the manifestations of the favors of God.

Necessarily there will be some who are defective amongst men, but it is our duty to enable them by kind methods of guidance and teaching to become perfected. Some will be found who are morally sick; they should be treated in order that they may be healed. Others are immature and like children; they must be trained and educated so that they may become wise and mature. Those who are asleep must be awakened; the indifferent must become mindful and attentive. But all this must be accomplished in the spirit of kindness and love and not by strife, antagonism nor in a spirit of hostility and hatred, for this is contrary to the good pleasure of God. That which is acceptable in the sight of God is love. Love is, in reality, the first effulgence of Divinity and the greatest splendor of God.

O Thou compassionate Lord, Thou Who art generous and able! We are servants of Thine sheltered beneath Thy providence. Cast Thy glance of favor upon us. Give light to our eyes, hearing to our ears, and understanding and love to our hearts. Render our souls joyous and happy through Thy glad tidings. O Lord! Point out to us the pathway of Thy kingdom and resuscitate all of us through the breaths of the Holy Spirit. Bestow upon us life everlasting and confer upon us never-ending honor. Unify mankind and illumine the world of humanity. May we all follow Thy pathway, long for Thy good pleasure and seek the mysteries of Thy kingdom. O God! Unite us and connect our hearts with Thine indissoluble bond. Verily, Thou art the Giver, Thou art the Kind One and Thou art the Almighty.

1 September 1912

––––––––––––––––––

TALK AT HOME OF MR. AND MRS. WILLIAM SUTHERLAND MAXWELL

––––––––––––––––––

716 Pine Avenue West
Montreal, Canada

From Stenographic Notes

I am exceedingly happy to meet you. Praise be to God! I see before me souls who have unusual capability and the power of spiritual advancement. In reality, the people of this continent possess great capacity; they are the cause of my happiness, and I ever pray that God may confirm and assist them to progress in all the degrees of existence. As they have advanced along material lines, may they develop in idealistic degrees, for material advancement is fruitless without spiritual progress and not productive of everlasting results. For example, no matter how much the physical body of man is trained and developed, there will be no real progression in the human station unless the mind correspondingly advances. No matter how much man may acquire material virtues, he will not be able to realize and express the highest possibilities of life without spiritual graces. God has created all earthly things under a law of progression in material degrees, but He has created man and endowed him with powers of advancement toward spiritual and transcendental kingdoms. He has not created material phenomena after His own image and likeness, but He has created man after that image and with potential power to attain that likeness. He has distinguished man above all other created things. All created things except man are captives of nature and the sense world, but in man there has been created an ideal power by which he may perceive intellectual or spiritual realities. He has brought forth everything necessary for the life of this world, but man is a creation intended for the reflection of divine virtues. Consider that the highest type of creation below man is the animal, which is superior to all degrees of life except man. Manifestly, the animal has been created for the life of this world. Its highest virtue is to express excellence in the material plane of existence. The animal is perfect when its body is healthy and its physical senses are whole. When it is characterized by the attributes of physical health, when its physical forces are in working order, when food and surrounding conditions minister to its needs, it has attained the ultimate perfection of its kingdom. But man does not depend upon these things for his virtues. No matter how perfect his health and physical powers, if that is all, he has not yet risen above the degree of a perfect animal. Beyond and above this, God has opened the doors of ideal virtues and attainments before the face of man. He has created in his being the mysteries of the divine Kingdom. He has bestowed upon him the power of intellect so that through the attribute of reason, when fortified by the Holy Spirit, he may penetrate and discover ideal realities and become informed of the mysteries of the world of significances. As this power to penetrate the ideal knowledges is superhuman, supernatural, man becomes the collective center of spiritual as well as material forces so that the divine spirit may manifest itself in his being, the effulgences of the Kingdom shine within the sanctuary of his heart, the signs of the attributes and perfections of God reveal themselves in a newness of life, the everlasting glory and eternal existence be attained, the knowledge of God illumine, and the mysteries of the realm of might be unsealed.

Man is like unto this lamp, but the effulgences of the Kingdom are like the rays of the lamp. Man is like unto the glass, but spiritual splendors are like unto the light within the glass. No matter how translucent the glass may be, as long as there is no light within, it remains dark. Likewise, man, no matter how much he advances in material accomplishments, will remain like the glass without light if he is deprived of the spiritual virtues. Material virtues are like unto a perfect body, but this body is in need of the spirit. No matter how handsome and perfect the body may be, if it is deprived of the spirit and its animus, it is dead. But when that same body is affiliated with the spirit and expressing life, perfection and virtue become realized in it. Deprived of the Holy Spirit and its bounties, man is spiritually dead.

Children, for instance, no matter how good and pure, no matter how healthy their bodies, are, nevertheless, considered imperfect because the power of intellect is not fully manifest in them. When the intellectual power fully displays its influences and they attain to the age of maturity, they are considered as perfect. Likewise, man, no matter how much he may advance in worldly affairs and make progress in material civilization, is imperfect unless he is quickened by the bounties of the Holy Spirit; for it is evident that until he receives that divine impetus he is ignorant and deprived. For this reason Jesus Christ said, "Except a man be born of water and of the Spirit, he cannot enter into the kingdom of God." By this Christ meant that unless man is released from the material world, freed from the captivity of materialism and receiving a portion of the bounties of the spiritual world, he shall be deprived of the bestowals and favors of the Kingdom of God, and the utmost we can say of him is that he is a perfect animal. No one can rightly call him a man. In another place He said, "That which is born of the flesh is flesh; and that which is born of the Spirit is spirit." The meaning of this is that if man is a captive of nature, he is like unto an animal because he is only a body physically born—that is, he belongs to the world of matter and remains subject to the law and control of nature. But if he is baptized with the Holy Spirit, if he is freed from the bondage of nature, released from animalistic tendencies and advanced in the human realm, he is fitted to enter into the divine Kingdom. The world of the Kingdom is the realm of divine bestowals and the bounties of God. It is attainment of the highest virtues of humanity; it is nearness to God; it is capacity to receive the bounties of the ancient Lord. When man advances to this station, he attains the second birth. Before his first or physical

birth man was in the world of the matrix. He had
no knowledge of this world; his eyes could not see;
his ears could not hear. When he was born from the
world of the matrix, he beheld another world. The
sun was shining with its splendors, the moon radiant in the heavens, the stars twinkling in the expan-
sive firmament, the seas surging, trees verdant and
green, all kinds of creatures enjoying life here, infinite
bounties prepared for him. In the world of the matrix
none of these things existed. In that world he had no
knowledge of this vast range of existence; nay, rather,
he would have denied the reality of this world. But after his birth he began to open his eyes and behold the
wonders of this illimitable universe. Similarly, as long
as man is in the matrix of the human world, as long
as he is the captive of nature, he is out of touch and
without knowledge of the universe of the Kingdom.
If he attains rebirth while in the world of nature, he
will become informed of the divine world. He will
observe that another and a higher world exists. Wonderful bounties descend; eternal life awaits; everlasting glory surrounds him. All the signs of reality and
greatness are there. He will see the lights of God. All
these experiences will be his when he is born out of
the world of nature into the divine world. Therefore,
for the perfect man there are two kinds of birth: the
first, physical birth, is from the matrix of the mother;
the second, or spiritual birth, is from the world of
nature. In both he is without knowledge of the new

world of existence he is entering. Therefore, rebirth means his release from the captivity of nature, freedom from attachment to this mortal and material life. This is the second, or spiritual, birth of which Jesus Christ spoke in the Gospels.

The majority of people are captives in the matrix of nature, submerged in the sea of materiality. We must pray that they may be reborn, that they may attain insight and spiritual hearing, that they may receive the gift of another heart, a new transcendent power, and in the eternal world the unending bestowal of divine bounties.

Today the world of humanity is walking in darkness because it is out of touch with the world of God. That is why we do not see the signs of God in the hearts of men. The power of the Holy Spirit has no influence. When a divine spiritual illumination becomes manifest in the world of humanity, when divine instruction and guidance appear, then enlightenment follows, a new spirit is realized within, a new power descends, and a new life is given. It is like the birth from the animal kingdom into the kingdom of man. When man acquires these virtues, the oneness of the world of humanity will be revealed, the banner of international peace will be upraised, equality between all mankind will be realized, and the Orient and Occident will become one. Then will the justice of God become manifest, all humanity will appear as the members of one family, and every member of that family will be consecrated to cooperation and mutual assistance. The lights of the love of God will shine; eternal happiness will be unveiled; everlasting joy and spiritual delight will be attained.

I will pray, and you must pray, likewise, that such heavenly bounty may be realized; that strife and enmity may be banished, warfare and bloodshed taken away; that hearts may attain ideal communication and that all people may drink from the same fountain. May they receive their knowledge from the same divine source. May all hearts become illumined with the rays of the Sun of Reality; may all of them enter the university of God, acquire spiritual virtues and seek for themselves heavenly bounties. Then this material, phenomenal world will become the mirror of the world of God, and within this pure mirror the divine virtues of the realm of might will be reflected.

27 August 1912

TALK AT
METAPHYSICAL
CLUB

Boston, Massachusetts

Notes by Edna McKinney

U pon the faces of those present I behold the expression of thoughtfulness and wisdom; therefore, I shall discourse upon a subject involving one of the divine questions, a question of religious and metaphysical importance—namely, the progressive and perpetual motion of elemental atoms throughout the various degrees of phenomena and the kingdoms of existence. It will be demonstrated and become evident that the origin and outcome of phenomena are identical and that there is an essential oneness in all existing things. This is a subtle principle appertaining to divine philosophy and requiring close analysis and attention.

The elemental atoms which constitute all phenomenal existence and being in this illimitable universe are in perpetual motion, undergoing continuous degrees of progression. For instance, let us conceive of an atom in the mineral kingdom progressing upward to the kingdom of the vegetable by entering into the composition and fibre of a tree or plant. From thence it is assimilated and transferred into the kingdom of the animal and finally, by the law and process of composition, becomes a part of the body of man. That is to say, it has traversed the intermediate degrees and stations of phenomenal existence, entering into the composition of various organisms in its journey. This motion or transference is progressive and perpetual, for after disintegration of the human body into which it has entered, it returns to the mineral kingdom whence it came and will continue to traverse the kingdoms of phenomena as before. This is an illustration designed to show that the constituent elemental atoms of phenomena undergo progressive transference and motion throughout the material kingdoms.

In its ceaseless progression and journeyings the atom becomes imbued with the virtues and powers of each degree or kingdom it traverses. In the degree of the mineral it possessed mineral affinities; in the kingdom of the vegetable it manifested the augmentative virtue or power of growth; in the animal organism it reflected the intelligence of that degree; and in the kingdom of man it was qualified with human attributes or virtues.

Furthermore, the forms and organisms of phenomenal being and existence in each of the kingdoms of the universe are myriad and numberless. The vegetable plane or kingdom, for instance, has its infinite variety of types and material structures of plant life—each distinct and different within itself, no two exactly alike in composition and detail—for there are no repetitions in nature, and the augmentative virtue cannot be confined to any given image or shape. Each leaf has its own particular identity—so to speak, its own individuality as a leaf. Therefore, each atom of

the innumerable elemental atoms, during its ceaseless motion through the kingdoms of existence as a
constituent of organic composition, not only becomes
imbued with the powers and virtues of the kingdoms
it traverses but also reflects the attributes and qualities of the forms and organisms of those kingdoms. As
each of these forms has its individual and particular
virtue, therefore, each elemental atom of the universe
has the opportunity of expressing an infinite variety of
those individual virtues. No atom is bereft or deprived
of this opportunity or right of expression. Nor can it
be said of any given atom that it is denied equal opportunities with other atoms; nay, all are privileged to
possess the virtues existent in these kingdoms and to
reflect the attributes of their organisms. In the various
transformations or passages from kingdom to kingdom the virtues expressed by the atoms in each degree
are peculiar to that degree. For example, in the world
of the mineral the atom does not express the vegetable
form and organism, and when through the process of
transmutation it assumes the virtues of the vegetable
degree, it does not reflect the attributes of animal organisms, and so on.

It is evident, then, that each elemental atom of the
universe is possessed of a capacity to express all the
virtues of the universe. This is a subtle and abstract realization. Meditate upon it, for within it lies the true
explanation of pantheism. From this point of view
and perception pantheism is a truth, for every atom

in the universe possesses or reflects all the virtues of life, the manifestation of which is effected through change and transformation. Therefore, the origin and outcome of phenomena is, verily, the omnipresent God; for the reality of all phenomenal existence is through Him. There is neither reality nor the manifestation of reality without the instrumentality of God. Existence is realized and possible through the bounty of God, just as the ray or flame emanating from this lamp is realized through the bounty of the lamp, from which it originates. Even so, all phenomena are realized through the divine bounty, and the explanation of true pantheistic statement and principle is that the phenomena of the universe find realization through the one power animating and dominating all things, and all things are but manifestations of its energy and bounty. The virtue of being and existence is through no other agency. Therefore, in the words of Bahá'u'lláh, the first teaching is the oneness of the world of humanity.

When the man who is spiritually sagacious and possessed of insight views the world of humanity, he will observe that the lights of the divine bounty are flooding all mankind, just as the lights of the sun shed their splendor upon all existing things. All phenomena of material existence are revealed through the ray emanating from the sun. Without light nothing would be visible. Similarly, all phenomena in the inner world of reality receive the bounties of God from the source of divine bestowal. This human plane, or kingdom, is one creation, and all souls are the signs and traces of the divine bounty. In this plane there are no exceptions; all have been recipients of their bestowals through the heavenly bounty. Can you find a soul bereft of the nearness of God? Can you find one whom God has deprived of its daily sustenance? This is impossible. God is kind and loving to all, and all are manifestations of the divine bounty. This is the oneness of the world of humanity.

But some souls are weak; we must endeavor to strengthen them. Some are ignorant, uninformed of the bounties of God; we must strive to make them knowing. Some are ailing; we must seek to restore them to health. Some are immature as children; they must be trained and assisted to attain maturity. We nurse the sick in tenderness and the kindly spirit of love; we do not despise them because they are ill. Therefore, we must exercise extreme patience, sympathy and love toward all mankind, considering no soul as rejected. If we look upon a soul as rejected, we have disobeyed the teachings of God. God is loving to all. Shall we be unjust or unkind to anyone? Is this allowable in the sight of God? God provides for all. Is it befitting for us to prevent the flow of His merciful provisions for mankind? God has created all in His image and likeness. Shall we manifest hatred for His creatures and servants? This would be contrary to the will of God and according to the will of Satan, by which we mean the natural inclinations of the lower nature. This lower nature in man is symbolized as Satan—the evil ego within us, not an evil personality outside.

Bahá'u'lláh teaches that the foundations of the divine religion are one reality which does not admit of multiplicity or division. Therefore, the commandments and teachings of God are one. The religious differences and divisions which exist in the world are due to blind imitations of forms without knowledge or investigation of the fundamental divine reality which underlies all the religions. Inasmuch as these imitations of ancestral forms are various, dissensions have arisen among the people of religion. Therefore, it is necessary to free mankind from this subjection to blind belief by pointing the way of guidance to reality itself, which is the only basis of unity.

Bahá'u'lláh says that religion must be conducive to love and unity. If it proves to be the source of hatred and enmity, its absence is preferable; for the will and law of God is love, and love is the bond between human hearts. Religion is the light of the world. If it is made the cause of darkness through human misunderstanding and ignorance, it would be better to do without it.

Religion must conform to science and reason; otherwise, it is superstition. God has created man in order that he may perceive the verity of existence and endowed him with mind or reason to discover truth. Therefore, scientific knowledge and religious belief must be conformable to the analysis of this divine faculty in man.

Prejudices of all kinds—whether religious, racial, patriotic or political—are destructive of divine foundations in man. All the warfare and bloodshed in human history have been the outcome of prejudice. This earth is one home and native land. God has created mankind with equal endowment and right to live upon the earth. As a city is the home of all its inhabitants although each may have his individual place of residence therein, so the earth's surface is one wide native land or home for all races of humankind. Racial prejudice or separation into nations such as French, German, American and so on is unnatural and proceeds from human motive and ignorance. All are the children and servants of God. Why should we be separated by artificial and imaginary boundaries? In the animal kingdom the doves flock together in harmony and agreement. They have no prejudices. We are human and superior in intelligence. Is it befitting that lower creatures should manifest virtues which lack expression in man?

Bahá'u'lláh has proclaimed and promulgated the foundation of international peace. For thousands of years men and nations have gone forth to the battlefield to settle their differences. The cause of this has been ignorance and degeneracy. Praise be to God! In this radiant century minds have developed, perceptions have become keener, eyes are illumined and ears attentive. Therefore, it will be impossible for war to continue. Consider human ignorance and inconsistency. A man who kills another man is punished by execution, but a military genius who kills one hundred thousand of his fellow creatures is immortalized as a hero. One man steals a small sum of money and is imprisoned as a thief. Another pillages a whole country and is honored as a patriot and conqueror. A single falsehood brings reproach and censure, but the wiles of politicians and diplomats excite the admiration and praise of a nation. Consider the ignorance and inconsistency of mankind. How darkened and savage are the instincts of humanity!

Bahá'u'lláh has announced that no matter how far the world of humanity may advance in material civilization, it is nevertheless in need of spiritual virtues and the bounties of God. The spirit of man is not illumined and quickened through material sources. It is not resuscitated by investigating phenomena of the world of matter. The spirit of man is in need of the protection of the Holy Spirit. Just as he advances by progressive stages from the mere physical world of being into the intellectual realm, so must he develop upward in moral attributes and spiritual graces. In the process of this attainment he is ever in need of the bestowals of the Holy Spirit. Material development may be likened to the glass of a lamp, whereas divine virtues and spiritual susceptibilities are the light within the glass. The lamp chimney is worthless without the light; likewise, man in his material condition requires the radiance and vivification of the divine graces and merciful attributes. Without the presence of the Holy Spirit he is lifeless. Although physically and mentally alive, he is spiritually dead. Christ announced, "That which is born of the flesh is flesh; and that which is born of the Spirit is spirit," meaning that man must be born again. As the babe is born into the light of this physical world, so must the physical and intellectual man be born into the light of the world of Divinity. In the matrix of the mother the unborn child was deprived and unconscious of the world of material existence, but after its birth it beheld the wonders and beauties of a new realm of life and being. In the world of the matrix it was utterly ignorant and unable to conceive of these new conditions, but after its transformation it discovers the radiant sun, trees, flowers and an infinite range of blessings and bounties awaiting it. In the human plane and kingdom man is a captive of nature and ignorant of the divine world until born of the breaths of the Holy Spirit out of physical conditions of limitation and deprivation. Then he beholds the reality of the spiritual realm and Kingdom, realizes the narrow restrictions of the mere human world of existence and becomes conscious of the unlimited and infinite glories of the world of God. Therefore, no matter how man may advance upon the physical and intellectual plane, he is ever in need of the boundless virtues of Divinity, the protection of the Holy Spirit and the face of God.

24 May 1912

TALK AT
FREE RELIGIOUS
ASSOCIATION,
OR
UNITARIAN
CONFERENCE

Boston, Massachusetts

From Stenographic Notes

Creation is the expression of motion. Motion is life. A moving object is a living object, whereas that which is motionless and inert is as dead. All created forms are progressive in their planes, or kingdoms of existence, under the stimulus of the power or spirit of life. The universal energy is dynamic. Nothing is stationary in the material world of outer phenomena or in the inner world of intellect and consciousness.

Religion is the outer expression of the divine reality. Therefore, it must be living, vitalized, moving and progressive. If it be without motion and nonprogressive, it is without the divine life; it is dead. The divine institutes are continuously active and evolutionary; therefore, the revelation of them must be progressive and continuous. All things are subject to reformation. This is a century of life and renewal. Sciences and arts, industry and invention have been reformed. Law and ethics have been reconstituted, reorganized. The world of thought has been regenerated. Sciences of former ages and philosophies of the past are useless today. Present exigencies demand new methods of solution; world problems are without precedent. Old ideas and modes of thought are fast becoming obsolete. Ancient laws and archaic ethical systems will not meet the requirements of modern conditions, for this is clearly the century of a new life, the century of the revelation of reality and, therefore, the greatest of all centuries. Consider how the scientific developments of fifty years have surpassed and eclipsed the knowledge and achievements of all the former ages combined. Would the announcements and theories of ancient astronomers explain our present knowledge of the suns and planetary systems? Would the mask of obscurity which beclouded medieval centuries meet the demand for clear-eyed vision and understanding which characterizes the world today? Will the despotism of former governments answer the call for freedom which has risen from the heart of humanity in this cycle of illumination? It is evident that no vital results are now forthcoming from the customs, institutions and standpoints of the past. In view of this, shall blind imitations of ancestral forms and theological interpretations continue to guide and control the religious life and spiritual development of humanity today? Shall man, gifted with the power of reason, unthinkingly follow and adhere to dogma, creeds and hereditary beliefs which will not bear the analysis of reason in this century of effulgent reality? Unquestionably this will not satisfy men of science, for when they find premise or conclusion contrary to present standards of proof and without real foundation, they reject that which has been formerly accepted as standard and correct and move forward from new foundations.

The divine Prophets have revealed and founded religion. They have laid down certain laws and heavenly principles for the guidance of mankind. They have taught and promulgated the knowledge of God, established praiseworthy ethical ideals and inculcated the highest standards of virtues in the human world. Gradually these heavenly teachings and foundations of reality have been beclouded by human interpretations and dogmatic imitations of ancestral beliefs. The essential realities, which the Prophets labored so hard to establish in human hearts and minds while undergoing ordeals and suffering tortures of persecution, have now well nigh vanished. Some of these heavenly Messengers have been killed, some imprisoned, all of Them despised and rejected while proclaiming the reality of Divinity. Soon after Their departure from this world, the essential truth of Their teachings was lost sight of and dogmatic imitations adhered to.

Inasmuch as human interpretations and blind imitations differ widely, religious strife and disagreement have arisen among mankind, the light of true religion has been extinguished and the unity of the world of humanity destroyed. The Prophets of God voiced the spirit of unity and agreement. They have been the Founders of divine reality. Therefore, if the nations of the world forsake imitations and investigate the reality underlying the revealed Word of God, they will agree and become reconciled. For reality is one and not multiple.

The nations and religions are steeped in blind and bigoted imitations. A man is a Jew because his father was a Jew. The Muslim follows implicitly the footsteps of his ancestors in belief and observance. The Buddhist is true to his heredity as a Buddhist. That is to say, they profess religious belief blindly and without investigation, making unity and agreement impossible. It is evident, therefore, that this condition will not be remedied without a reformation in the world of religion. In other words, the fundamental reality of the divine religions must be renewed, reformed, revoiced to mankind.

From the seed of reality religion has grown into a tree which has put forth leaves and branches, blossoms and fruit. After a time this tree has fallen into a condition of decay. The leaves and blossoms have withered and perished; the tree has become stricken and fruitless. It is not reasonable that man should hold to the old tree, claiming that its life forces are undiminished, its fruit unequaled, its existence eternal. The seed of reality must be sown again in human hearts in order that a new tree may grow therefrom and new divine fruits refresh the world. By this means the nations and peoples now divergent in religion will be brought into unity, imitations will be forsaken, and a universal brotherhood in reality itself will be established. Warfare and strife will cease among mankind; all will be reconciled as servants of God. For all are sheltered beneath the tree of His providence and mercy. God is kind to all; He is the giver of bounty to all alike, even as Jesus Christ has declared that God "sendeth rain on the just and on the unjust"—that is to say, the mercy of God is universal. All humanity is under the protection of His love and favor, and unto all He has pointed the way of guidance and progress. Progress is of two kinds: material and spiritual. The former is attained through observation of the surrounding existence and constitutes the foundation of civilization. Spiritual progress is through the breaths of the Holy Spirit and is the awakening of the conscious soul of man to perceive the reality of Divinity. Material progress ensures the happiness of the human world. Spiritual progress ensures the happiness and eternal continuance of the soul. The Prophets of God have founded the laws of divine civilization. They have been the root and fundamental source of all knowledge. They have established the principles of human brotherhood, of fraternity, which is of various kinds—such as the fraternity of family, of race, of nation and of ethical motives. These forms of fraternity, these bonds of brotherhood, are merely temporal and transient in association. They do not ensure harmony and are usually productive of disagreement. They do not prevent warfare and strife; on the contrary, they are selfish, restricted and fruitful causes of enmity and hatred among mankind. The spiritual brotherhood which is enkindled and established through the breaths of the Holy Spirit unites nations and removes the cause of warfare and strife. It transforms mankind into one great family and establishes the foundations of the oneness of humanity. It promulgates the spirit of international agreement and ensures universal peace. Therefore, we must investigate the foundation of this heavenly fraternity. We must forsake all imitations and promote the reality of the divine teachings. In accordance with these principles and actions and by the assistance of the Holy Spirit, both material and spiritual happiness shall become realized. Until all nations and peoples become united by the bonds of the Holy Spirit in this real fraternity, until national and international prejudices are effaced in the reality of this spiritual brotherhood, true progress, prosperity and lasting happiness will not be attained by man. This is the century of new and universal nationhood. Sciences have advanced; industries have progressed; politics have been reformed; liberty has been proclaimed; justice is awakening. This is the century of motion, divine stimulus and accomplishment, the century of human solidarity and altruistic service, the century of universal peace and the reality of the divine Kingdom.

28 OCTOBER 1911

———————————

BEAUTY
AND
HARMONY
IN DIVERSITY

———————————

PARIS, FRANCE

The Creator of all is One God.

From this same God all creation sprang into existence, and He is the one goal, towards which everything in nature yearns. This conception was embodied in the words of Christ, when He said, "I am the Alpha and the Omega, the beginning and the end." Man is the sum of Creation, and the Perfect Man is the expression of the complete thought of the Creator—the Word of God.

Consider the world of created beings, how varied and diverse they are in species, yet with one sole origin. All the differences that appear are those of outward form and color. This diversity of type is apparent throughout the whole of nature.

Behold a beautiful garden full of flowers, shrubs, and trees. Each flower has a different charm, a peculiar beauty, its own delicious perfume and beautiful color. The trees too, how varied are they in size, in growth, in foliage—and what different fruits they bear! Yet all these flowers, shrubs and trees spring from the self-same earth, the same sun shines upon them and the same clouds give them rain.

So it is with humanity. It is made up of many races, and its peoples are of different color, white, black, yellow, brown and red—but they all come from the same God, and all are servants to Him. This diversity among the children of men has unhappily not the same effect as it has among the vegetable creation, where the spirit shown is more harmonious. Among men exists the diversity of animosity, and it is this that causes war and hatred among the different nations of the world.

Differences which are only those of blood also cause them to destroy and kill one another. Alas! that this should still be so. Let us look rather at the beauty in diversity, the beauty of harmony, and learn a lesson from the vegetable creation. If you beheld a garden in which all the plants were the same as to form, color and perfume, it would not seem beautiful to you at all, but, rather, monotonous and dull. The garden which is pleasing to the eye and which makes the heart glad, is the garden in which are growing side by side flowers of every hue, form and perfume, and the joyous contrast of color is what makes for charm and beauty. So is it with trees. An orchard full of fruit trees is a delight; so is a plantation planted with many species of shrubs. It is just the diversity and variety that constitutes its charm; each flower, each tree, each fruit, beside being beautiful in itself, brings out by contrast the qualities of the others, and shows to advantage the special loveliness of each and all.

Thus should it be among the children of men! The diversity in the human family should be the cause of love and harmony, as it is in music where many different notes blend together in the making of a perfect chord. If you meet those of different race and color from yourself, do not mistrust them and withdraw yourself into your shell of conventionality, but rather be glad and show them kindness. Think of them as different colored roses growing in the beautiful garden of humanity, and rejoice to be among them.

Likewise, when you meet those whose opinions differ from your own, do not turn away your face from them. All are seeking truth, and there are many roads leading thereto. Truth has many aspects, but it remains always and forever one.

Do not allow difference of opinion, or diversity of thought to separate you from your fellowmen, or to be the cause of dispute, hatred and strife in your hearts.

Rather, search diligently for the truth and make all men your friends.

Every edifice is made of many different stones, yet each depends on the other to such an extent that if one were displaced the whole building would suffer; if one is faulty the structure is imperfect.

Bahá'u'lláh has drawn the circle of unity, He has made a design for the uniting of all the peoples, and for the gathering of them all under the shelter of the tent of universal unity. This is the work of the Divine Bounty, and we must all strive with heart and soul until we have the reality of unity in our midst, and as we work, so will strength be given unto us. Leave all thought of self, and strive only to be obedient and submissive to the Will of God. In this way only shall we become citizens of the Kingdom of God, and attain unto life everlasting.

4 December 1912

_____

TALK TO
THEOSOPHICAL
SOCIETY

_____

2228 BROADWAY
NEW YORK

Notes by Esther Foster

Those who are uninformed of the world of reality, who do not comprehend existing things, who are without perception of the inner truth of creation, who do not penetrate the real mysteries of material and spiritual phenomena and who possess only a superficial idea of universal life and being are but embodiments of pure ignorance. They believe only that which they have heard from their fathers and ancestors. Of themselves they have no hearing, no sight, no reason, no intellect; they rely solely upon tradition. Such persons imagine that the dominion of God is an accidental dominion, or Kingdom.

For instance, they believe that this world of existence was created six or seven thousand years ago, as if God did not reign before that time and had no creation before that period. They think that Divinity is accidental, for to them Divinity is dependent upon existing things, whereas, in reality, as long as there has been a God, there has been a creation. As long as there has been light, there have been recipients of that light, for light cannot become manifest unless those things which perceive and appreciate it exist. The world of Divinity presupposes creation, presupposes recipients of bounty, presupposes the existence of worlds. No Divinity can be conceived as separate from creation, for otherwise it would be like imagining an empire without a people. A king must needs have a kingdom, must needs have an army and subjects. Is it possible to be a king and have no country, no army, no subjects? This is an absurdity. If we say that there was a time when there was no country, no army and no subjects, how then could there have been a king and ruler? For these things are essential to a king.

Consequently, just as the reality of Divinity never had a beginning—that is, God has ever been a Creator, God has ever been a Provider, God has ever been a Quickener, God has ever been a Bestower—so there never has been a time when the attributes of God have not had expression. The sun is the sun because of its rays, because of its heat. Were we to conceive of a time when there was a sun without heat and light, it would imply that there had been no sun at all and that it became the sun afterward. So, likewise, if we say there was a time when God had no creation or created beings, a time when there were no recipients of His bounties and that His names and attributes had not been manifested, this would be equivalent to a complete denial of Divinity, for it would mean that Divinity is accidental. To explain it still more clearly, if we think that fifty thousand years ago or one hundred thousand years ago there was no creation, that there were then no worlds, no human beings, no animals, this thought of ours would mean that previous to that period there was no Divinity. If we should say that there was a time when there was a king but there were no subjects, no army, no country for him to rule over, it would really be asserting that there was a time when no king existed and that the king is accidental. It is, therefore, evident that inasmuch as the reality of Divinity is without a beginning, creation is also without a beginning. This is as clear as the sun. When we contemplate this vast machinery of omnipresent power, perceive this illimitable space and its innumerable worlds, it will become evident to us that the lifetime of this infinite creation is more than six thousand years; nay, it is very, very ancient.

Notwithstanding this, we read in Genesis in the Old Testament that the lifetime of creation is but six thousand years. This has an inner meaning and significance; it is not to be taken literally. For instance, it is said in the Old Testament that certain things were created in the first day. The narrative shows that at that time the sun was not yet created. How could we conceive of a day if no sun existed in the heavens? For the day depends upon the light of the sun. Inasmuch as the sun had not been made, how could the first day be realized? Therefore, these statements have significances other than literal.

To be brief: Our purpose is to show that the divine sovereignty, the Kingdom of God, is an ancient sovereignty, that it is not an accidental sovereignty, just as a kingdom presupposes the existence of subjects, of an army, of a country; for otherwise the state of dominion, authority and kingdom cannot be conceived of. Therefore, if we should imagine that the creation is accidental, we would be forced to admit that the

Creator is accidental, whereas the divine bounty is ever flowing, and the rays of the Sun of Truth are continuously shining. No cessation is possible to the divine bounty, just as no cessation is possible to the rays of the sun. This is clear and obvious.

Thus there have been many holy Manifestations of God. One thousand years ago, two hundred thousand years ago, one million years ago, the bounty of God was flowing, the radiance of God was shining, the dominion of God was existing.

Why do these holy Manifestations of God appear? What is the wisdom and purpose of Their coming? What is the outcome of Their mission? It is evident that human personality appears in two aspects: the image or likeness of God, and the aspect of Satan. The human reality stands between these two: the divine and the satanic. It is manifest that beyond this material body, man is endowed with another reality, which is the world of exemplars constituting the heavenly body of man. In speaking, man says, "I saw," "I spoke," "I went." Who is this I? It is obvious that this I is different from this body. It is clear that when man is thinking, it is as though he were consulting with some other person. With whom is he consulting? It is evident that it is another reality, or one aside from this body, with whom he enters into consultation when he thinks, "Shall I do this work or not?" "What will be the result of my doing this?" Or when he questions the other reality, "What is the objection to this work if I do it?" And then that reality in man communicates its opinion to him concerning the point at issue. Therefore, that reality in man is clearly and obviously other than his body—an ego with which man enters into consultation and whose opinion man seeks.

Often a man makes up his mind positively about a matter; for instance, he determines to undertake a journey. Then he thinks it over—that is, he consults his inner reality—and finally concludes that he will give up his journey. What has happened? Why did he abandon his original purpose? It is evident that he has consulted his inner reality, which expresses to him the disadvantages of such a journey; therefore, he defers to that reality and changes his original intention.

Furthermore, man sees in the world of dreams. He travels in the East; he travels in the West; although his body is stationary, his body is here. It is that reality in him which makes the journey while the body sleeps. There is no doubt that a reality exists other than the outward, physical reality. Again, for instance, a person is dead, is buried in the ground. Afterward, you see him in the world of dreams and speak with him, although his body is interred in the earth. Who is the person you see in your dreams, talk to and who also speaks with you? This again proves that there is another reality different from the physical one which dies and is buried. Thus it is certain that in man there is a reality which is not the physical body. Sometimes the body becomes weak, but that other reality is in its own normal state. The body goes to sleep, becomes as one dead; but that reality is moving about, comprehending things, expressing them and is even conscious of itself.

This other and inner reality is called the heavenly body, the ethereal form which corresponds to this body. This is the conscious reality which discovers the inner meaning of things, for the outer body of man does not discover anything. The inner ethereal reality grasps the mysteries of existence, discovers scientific truths and indicates their technical application. It discovers electricity, produces the telegraph, the telephone and opens the door to the world of arts. If the outer material body did this, the animal would, likewise, be able to make scientific and wonderful discoveries, for the animal shares with man all physical powers and limitations. What, then, is that power which penetrates the realities of existence and which is not to be found in the animal? It is the inner reality which comprehends things, throws light upon the mysteries of life and being, discovers the heavenly Kingdom, unseals the mysteries of God and differentiates man from the brute. Of this there can be no doubt.

As we have before indicated, this human reality stands between the higher and the lower in man, between the world of the animal and the world of Divinity. When the animal proclivity in man becomes predominant, he sinks even lower than the brute. When the heavenly powers are triumphant in his nature, he becomes the noblest and most superior being in the world of creation. All the imperfections found in the animal are found in man. In him there is antagonism, hatred and selfish struggle for existence; in his nature lurk jealousy, revenge, ferocity, cunning, hypocrisy, greed, injustice and tyranny. So to speak, the reality of man is clad in the outer garment of the animal, the habiliments of the world of nature, the world of darkness, imperfections and unlimited baseness.

On the other hand, we find in him justice, sincerity, faithfulness, knowledge, wisdom, illumination, mercy and pity, coupled with intellect, comprehension, the power to grasp the realities of things and the ability to penetrate the truths of existence. All these great perfections are to be found in man. Therefore, we say that man is a reality which stands between light and darkness. From this standpoint his nature is threefold: animal, human and divine. The animal nature is darkness; the heavenly is light in light.

The holy Manifestations of God come into the world to dispel the darkness of the animal, or physical, nature of man, to purify him from his imperfections in order that his heavenly and spiritual nature may become quickened, his divine qualities awakened, his perfections visible, his potential powers revealed and all the virtues of the world of humanity latent within him may come to life. These holy Manifestations of God are the Educators and Trainers of the world of existence, the Teachers of the world of humanity. They liberate man from the darkness of the world of nature, deliver him from despair, error, ignorance, imperfections and all evil qualities. They clothe him in the garment of perfections and exalted virtues. Men are ignorant; the Manifestations of God make them wise. They are animalistic; the Manifestations make them human. They are savage and cruel; the Manifestations lead them into kingdoms of light and love. They are unjust; the Manifestations cause them to become just. Man is selfish; They sever him from self and desire. Man is haughty; They make him meek, humble and friendly. He is earthly; They make him heavenly. Men are material; the Manifestations transform them into divine semblance. They are immature children; the Manifestations develop them into maturity. Man is poor; They endow him with wealth. Man is base, treacherous and mean; the Manifestations of God uplift him into dignity, nobility and loftiness.

These holy Manifestations liberate the world of humanity from the imperfections which beset it and cause men to appear in the beauty of heavenly perfections. Were it not for the coming of these holy Manifestations of God, all mankind would be found on the plane of the animal. They would remain darkened and ignorant like those who have been denied schooling and who never had a teacher or trainer. Undoubtedly, such unfortunates will continue in their condition of need and deprivation.

If the mountains, hills and plains of the material world are left wild and uncultivated under the rule of nature, they will remain an unbroken wilderness, no fruitful tree to be found anywhere upon them. A true cultivator changes this forest and jungle into a garden, training its trees to bring forth fruit and causing flowers to grow in place of thorns and thistles. The holy Manifestations are the ideal Gardeners of human souls, the divine Cultivators of human hearts. The world of existence is but a jungle of disorder and confusion, a state of nature producing nothing but fruitless, useless trees. The ideal Gardeners train these wild, uncultivated human trees, cause them to become fruitful, water and cultivate them day by day so that they adorn the world of existence and continue to flourish in the utmost beauty.

Consequently, we cannot say that the divine bounty has ceased, that the glory of Divinity is exhausted or the Sun of Truth sunk into eternal sunset, into that darkness which is not followed by light, into that night which is not followed by a sunrise and dawn, into that death which is not followed by life, into that error which is not followed by truth. Is it conceivable that the Sun of Reality should sink into an eternal darkness? No! The sun was created in order that it may shed light upon the world and train all the kingdoms of existence. How then can the ideal Sun of Truth, the Word of God, set forever? For this would mean the cessation of the divine bounty, and the divine bounty by its very nature is continuous and ceaseless. Its sun is ever shining; its cloud is ever producing rain; its breezes are ever blowing; its bestowals are all-comprehending; its gifts are ever perfect. Consequently, we must always anticipate, always be hopeful and pray to God that He will send unto us His holy Manifestations in Their most perfect might, with the divine penetrative power of His Word, so that these heavenly Ones may be distinguished above all other beings in every respect, in every attribute, just as the glorious sun is distinguished above all stars.

Although the stars are scintillating and brilliant, the sun is superior to them in luminous effulgence. Similarly, these holy, divine Manifestations are and must always be distinguished above all other beings in every attribute of glory and perfection in order that it may be proven that the Manifestation is the true Teacher and real Trainer; that He is the Sun of Truth, endowed with a supreme splendor and reflecting the beauty of God. Otherwise, it is not possible for us to train one human individual and then after training him, believe in him and accept him as the holy Manifestation of Divinity. The real Manifestation of God must be endowed with divine knowledge and not dependent upon learning acquired in schools. He must be the Educator, not the educated; His standard, intuition instead of tuition. He must be perfect and not imperfect, great and glorious instead of being weak and impotent. He must be wealthy in the riches of the spiritual world and not indigent. In a word, the holy, divine Manifestation of God must be distinguished above all others of mankind in every aspect and qualification in order that He may be able to train effectively the human body politic, eliminate the darkness enshrouding the human world, uplift humanity from a lower to a higher kingdom, be able through the penetrative power of His Word to promote and spread broadcast the beneficent message of universal peace among men, bring about the unification of mankind in religious belief through a manifest divine power, harmonize all sects and denominations and convert all native lands and nationalities into one native land and fatherland.

It is our hope that the bounties of God will encompass us all, the gifts of the divine become manifest, the lights of the Sun of Truth illumine our eyes, inspire our hearts, convey to our souls cheerful glad tidings of God, cause our thoughts to become lofty and our efforts to be productive of glorious results. In a word, it is our hope that we may attain to that which is the summit of human aspirations and wishes.

I have been in America nine months and have traveled to all the large cities, speaking before various assemblages, proclaiming to them the oneness of the world of humanity, summoning all to union, harmony and oneness. I have indeed received the greatest kindness from the American people. I look upon them as a noble nation, capable of every perfection. Tomorrow I am going away to Europe, and now I bid farewell to you all, seeking for you the divine mercy, the eternal glory and everlasting life; and I pray that you may attain the highest station of humanity. I am greatly pleased with this meeting. My happiness is great. I shall never forget you. You shall always live in my thought. I shall always pray and supplicate before the Kingdom of God and seek heavenly blessings for you.

All of the talks compiled in this volume come from *Paris Talks: Addresses Given by 'Abdu'l-Bahá in 1911* (Bahá'í Publishing, 2011) and *The Promulgation of Universal Peace: Talks Delivered by 'Abdu'l-Bahá during His Visit to the United States and Canada in 1912* (Bahá'í Publishing, 2012).

For more information about the Bahá'í Faith,
or to contact Bahá'ís near you,
visit http://www.bahai.us/
or call
1-800-22-UNITE

Bahá'í
PUBLISHING
AND THE BAHÁ'Í FAITH

Bahá'í Publishing produces books based on the teachings of the Bahá'í Faith. Founded over 160 years ago, the Bahá'í Faith has spread to some 235 nations and territories and is now accepted by more than five million people. The word "Bahá'í" means "follower of Bahá'u'lláh." Bahá'u'lláh, the founder of the Bahá'í Faith, asserted that He is the Messenger of God for all of humanity in this day. The cornerstone of His teachings is the establishment of the spiritual unity of humankind, which will be achieved by personal transformation and the application of clearly identified spiritual principles. Bahá'ís also believe that there is but one religion and that all the Messengers of God—among them Abraham, Zoroaster, Moses, Krishna, Buddha, Jesus, and Muḥammad—have progressively revealed its nature. Together, the world's great religions are expressions of a single, unfolding divine plan. Human beings, not God's Messengers, are the source of religious divisions, prejudices, and hatreds.

The Bahá'í Faith is not a sect or denomination of another religion, nor is it a cult or a social movement. Rather, it is a globally recognized independent world religion founded on new books of scripture revealed by Bahá'u'lláh.

Bahá'í Publishing is an imprint of the National Spiritual Assembly of the Bahá'ís of the United States.

OTHER BOOKS AVAILABLE FROM BAHÁ'Í PUBLISHING

'Abdu'l-Bahá in America
Robert H. Stockman
$18.00 U.S. / $20.00 CAN
Trade Paper
ISBN 978-1-931847-97-1

The amazing account of the journey of 'Abdu'l-Bahá across much of the United States to share the message of the oneness of humanity and the principles of universal peace.

'Abdu'l-Bahá in America is the account of the journey of 'Abdu'l-Bahá, eldest son of Bahá'u'lláh and appointed head of the Bahá'í Faith after his father's passing, across much of the United States in 1912. His exhausting yet exhilarating 239-day trek from coast to coast took him to fifty cities and towns, where he delivered up to four talks a day—about four hundred total—to approximately ninety-three thousand people about Bahá'u'lláh's message of the oneness of humanity and the principles of universal peace. This historic visit to the United States planted the seeds that would take root and germinate into the present-day American Bahá'í community.

The author has meticulously researched the journey of 'Abdu'l-Bahá by combing through discourses as well as the diary of his traveling companion, which describes almost every major event during the journey as well as many private scenes and frank comments by 'Abdu'l-Bahá. The extensive research includes the examination of newspaper and magazine articles published at the time of this historic visit, as well as hundreds of pages of unpublished telegrams, letters, diaries, and memoirs.

Portals to Freedom
Howard Colby Ives
$16.00 U.S. / $18.00 CAN
Trade Paper
ISBN 978-1-931847-99-5

A personal memoir that deals with spiritual transformation, and brings to life in warm and intimate detail the historical figure of 'Abdu'l-Bahá.

Portals to Freedom is an intimate portrait of one of the most significant religious figures in recent history, 'Abdu'l-Bahá—the son and appointed successor of the Prophet of the Bahá'í Faith. Author Howard Colby Ives offers us a remarkably candid and honest description of his own personal spiritual search as a Unitarian minister struggling with questions of faith and spirituality. His search ultimately led him to a discovery of the Bahá'í Faith just a short time before 'Abdu'l-Bahá arrived in North America in 1912 on a quest to share the teachings and vision of his father with the people of the West. In *Portals* we get not only Ives's personal reflections and inner struggles, but a fascinating eyewitness account of the words and actions of one who has been described by his Prophet-father as "the Mystery of God," is considered by Bahá'ís to be the perfect exemplar of the Faith's teachings, and who emerged from a lifetime of exile at the hands of the Ottoman Empire to travel tirelessly and share the Faith's message of unity in a profound and loving manner that touched the hearts of all with whom he came in contact.

Spirit of Faith
THE HUMAN SOUL
Bahá'í Publishing
$12.00 U.S. / $14.00 CAN
Hardcover
ISBN 978-1-61851-000-6

A collection of uplifting prayers and writings that focuses on the human soul for spiritual seekers of all faiths.

Spirit of Faith: The Human Soul is a compilation of writings and prayers that focus on the human soul and the qualities of this remarkable and unique aspect of our existence. Spiritual seekers of all faiths will relish these uplifting passages that offer a great deal of insight into the nature and significance of the human soul—a subject that has never been so extensively explored in the religious texts of the past. This collection contains writings from Bahá'u'lláh, the Báb, and 'Abdu'l-Bahá.

The *Spirit of Faith* series explores a range of topics—such as the unity of humanity, the eternal covenant of God, the promise of world peace, and much more—by taking an in-depth look at how the writings of the Bahá'í Faith view these issues. The series is designed to encourage readers of all faiths to think about spirituality, and to take time to pray and meditate on these important topics.

The Promulgation of Universal Peace
TALKS DELIVERED BY 'ABDU'L-BAHÁ
DURING HIS VISIT TO THE UNITED STATES
AND CANADA IN 1912
'Abdu'l-Bahá
$25.00 U.S. / $27.00 CAN
Hardcover
ISBN 978-1-931847-98-8

A special centenary edition marking the 100th anniversary of the talks delivered by 'Abdu'l-Bahá during his historic journey through North America in 1912.

The Promulgation of Universal Peace is a collection of 140 talks given by 'Abdu'l-Bahá—the son and appointed successor of Bahá'u'lláh, the Prophet and Founder of the Bahá'í Faith—during his extensive tour of North America in 1912. This compilation touches on a wide range of subjects including the coming of age of the human race, the oneness and continuity of the Prophets of God, and the oneness of religion as a social force for establishing world order and peace. These talks serve as a priceless resource for studying the language and personal example of one of the most significant religious figures in recent history.